Native Cultures in Alaska

LOOKING FORWARD, LOOKING BACK

Edited by Tricia Brown

ALASKA
NORTHWEST
BOOKS®

First published and copyright © 1996 by The Alaska Geographic Society® as Vol. 23, No. 2, *Native Cultures in Alaska*, an Alaska Geographic serial publication (ISSN 0361-1353), edited by Penny Rennick.

Note to the Reader: The northern aboriginal people of the United States and Canada hold varying preferences regarding the name of their group. The northern-tier First Nations people of Canada prefer to be called "Inuit," and may be offended by the use of the word "Eskimo." Meanwhile the Native Alaskan Eskimo groups—the Iñupiat, Yup'ik, and Siberian Yupik—refer to themselves as Eskimo. No offense is intended in the use of any term in this book.

Library of Congress Cataloging-in-Publication Data
  Native cultures in Alaska.
  Anchorage : Alaska Northwest Books, 2012.
0904
Alaska Northwest Books
    p. cm.
  Includes bibliographical references and index.
  ISBN 978-0-88240-756-2 (pbk.)
  ISBN 978-0-88240-902-3 (e-book)
  ISBN 978-0-88240-961-0 (hardbound)
1. Indians of North America—Alaska—History. 2. Indians of North America—Alaska—Social life and customs.

  E78.A3 N384 2012
  979.8004/97

                    2008042039

Alaska Northwest Books®
An imprint of

GRAPHIC ARTS
BOOKS®

P.O. Box 56118
Portland, OR 97238-6118
(503) 254-5591
www.graphicartsbooks.com

Design: Elizabeth Watson and Constance Bollen
Maps: Marge Mueller, Gray Mouse Graphics

Alaska Geographic is a nonprofit publisher, educator, and supporter of Alaska's parks, forests, and refuges. A portion of every purchase at Alaska Geographic bookstores directly supports educational and interpretive programs at Alaska's public lands. Learn more and become a supporting member at: www.alaskageographic.org

Your Connection to Alaska's Parks,
Forests, and Refuges

Alaska
Geographic

Cover photo: A Yup'ik woman with dance fans and regalia *(Chris Arend/Alaska Stock)*. **Front Cover (Inset): from left, Carla Schleusner, Chris Leask, and Melody Leask in their dance finery** *(Roy Corral)*. **Back Cover: Young Jerrald John discovers bear tracks along the Chandalar River, north of Arctic Village** *(Roy Corral)*. **Page 3: A dancer performs at Quyana Alaska, a multicultural celebration held annually during the Alaska Federation of Natives Convention** *(Roy Corral)*. **Page 4: A row of totem poles represents the Haida clans** *(Roy Corral)*.

Contents

7   **Introduction: Uniquely Alaskan**

10   **Map**

23   **Looking Forward, Looking Back**

41   **Unangaˆx (Aleut)**

Riding Ungiikan Home,

      by Barbara Švarný Carlson.......................48

55   **Sugpiaq (Alutiiq)**

Who Are We, Anyway? by Gordon Pullar 64

73   **Yup'ik**

Yup'ik Dance Masks: Stories of Culture......................82

Siberian Yupik..85

89   **Iñupiat**

A Time for Whaling, by Sheila Frankson...................100

105   **Athabascan**

People of the Yukon Flats, by Velma Wallis.............116

123   **Eyak**

133   **Tlingit**

Carving Traditions, by Nathan Jackson......................142

149   **Tsimshian**

157   **Haida**

Delores Churchill: The Weaver's Daughter.............164

168   **Bibliography**

170   **Index**

Introduction
Uniquely Alaskan

The first people to North America arrived many thousands of years ago. Today, many of their descendants still live in Alaska—people collectively known as Alaska Natives.

Alaska Natives share a common history of events that have shaped their modern existence and have become a political force with certain rights and privileges. They are the only indigenous people in the United States who were not relocated to reservations by the federal government. The single exception is the Tsimshian people, who emigrated to Annette Island from western Canada in 1887 and four years later requested reservation status for their adopted island from President Grover Cleveland. Other Alaska Natives still live, hunt, and fish on the same lands as did their ancestors. Many still speak their ancestral languages, perform ancestral dances, share ancestral stories, and practice age-old values handed down through generations.

Simultaneously, Alaska's first people are also fully engaged in the 21st-century world, working, embracing modern technology, and enjoying the benefits of a global economy. They struggle with the same problems as their non-Native neighbors, but increasingly are looking within their cultures for solutions. As Elders age and the body of traditional knowledge grows dimmer, maturing generations face new challenges in keeping their heritage alive.

Even so, Alaska Natives are not a single, homogeneous entity. Broadly identified by anthropologists as Aleuts, Eskimos, and Indians, Alaska Natives belong, more specifically, to one of twenty language and culture groups. Within those are particular village and tribal

Facing page: A modern Tsimshian woman wears regalia very similar to that of her ancestors. *(Jeff Schultz/ AlaskaStock.com)*

affiliations. And though many Natives have moved to Alaska's urban areas, each identifies with a different geographic region where their ancestors lived and where their home villages are today.

Elder S. Zeeder, Sr., of Kodiak often visits his boyhood home in Akiok. *(Roy Corral)*

This book takes a closer look at the rich and diverse cultures of Alaska's various Native groups, and how they continue cultural practices and activities within the context of contemporary society.

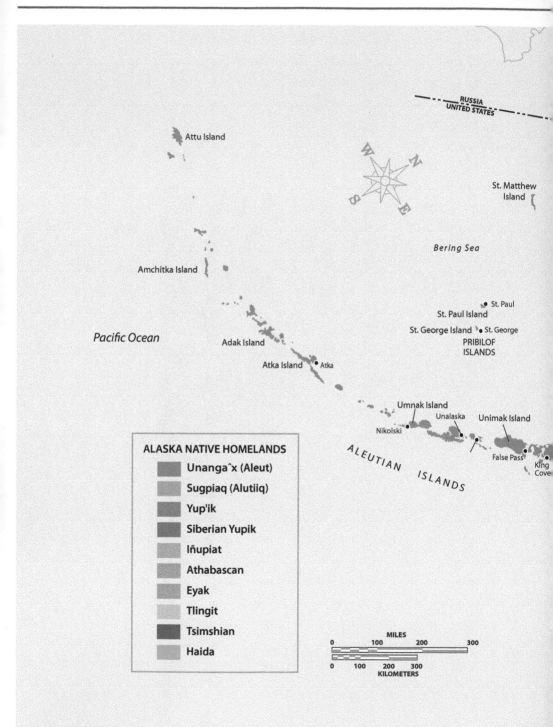

Attu Island

RUSSIA
UNITED STATES

St. Matthew
Island

Bering Sea

Amchitka Island

St. Paul
St. Paul Island

St. George Island • St. George
PRIBILOF
ISLANDS

Pacific Ocean

Adak Island

Atka Island • Atka

Umnak Island
Unalaska   Unimak Island
Nikolski

ALEUTIAN   ISLANDS

False Pass
King
Cove

ALASKA NATIVE HOMELANDS

- Unangaˆx (Aleut)
- Sugpiaq (Alutiiq)
- Yup'ik
- Siberian Yupik
- Iñupiat
- Athabascan
- Eyak
- Tlingit
- Tsimshian
- Haida

MILES
0   100   200   300

0   100   200   300
KILOMETERS

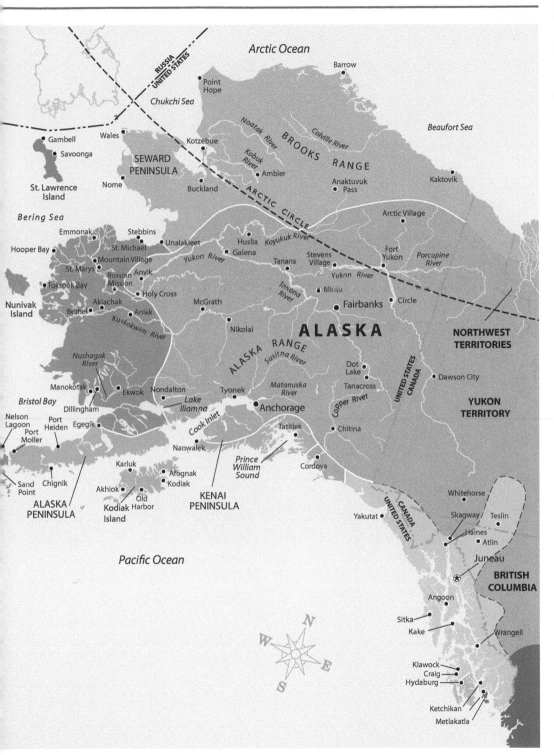

Traditional
Homeland
Unangaˆx

Attu was especially noted for its expert basket-weavers, including this woman photographed by Margaret Murie in the early 20th century. *(UAF-1990-3-2, Archives, Alaska and Polar Regions Collection, Margaret Murie Collection, Rasmuson Library, University of Alaska Fairbanks, Alaska)*

Below: A modern Attu-style basket using dyed rye grass. *(Courtesy Sharon Kay)*

Unangaˆx **(Aleut).** Pronounced *oo-NUNG-ah*, Unangaˆx means "people who go between the straits," and is the people's preferred term over "Aleut," the name given by Russians. Other forms of the name include Unangas and Unangan. The traditional lands of these expert seafarers were the Aleutian Islands and southern Alaska Peninsula. Two centuries ago, some Unangaˆx were resettled on the Pribilof Islands by Russian fur traders who forced Native men to assist in their fur seal harvest. The Native language is called *Unangam Tunuu.*

Sugpiaq (Alutiiq). Pronounced *SUG-pea-ak*, this plural self-descriptor is today gaining preference over *Alutiiq*, which, like *Aleut*, has Russian roots. These people settled throughout a wide, largely coastal region, including the Kodiak Island archipelago, Alaska Peninsula, Lower Cook Inlet, and Prince William Sound. In past times, segments of the population have been referred to as Aleut, Pacific Eskimo, Koniag Eskimo, and Chugach Eskimo. The Alutiiq language, *Sugt'stun*, is part of the Aleut-Eskimo linguistic family and is closely related to Yup'ik. Its two dialects are Koniag and Chugach.

Above: The "Married Couple" Sugpiak mask was collected from Alaska in the 1800s and taken to France. *(Sven Haakanson)*
The people fashioned rainproof garments from seal intestines, sewn in horizontal strips with sinew and sometimes decorated with beads, bird beaks, or bits of feathers, as shown in this 1919 photo from Kodiak Island. *(UAA-hmc-0186-volume6-5210, National Geographic Society. Katmai Expeditions. Photographs, 1913-1919 University of Alaska Anchorage, Archives & Manuscripts)*

Traditional Homeland Sugpiak

13

Siberian
Yupik

Yup'ik

Traditional
Homelands
Yup'ik

Yup'ik (YOU-pik). Throughout the Yukon–Kuskokwim Delta of southwestern Alaska, and along the Bering Sea and Bristol Bay coastlines, the Yup'ik people live in roughly sixty-eight communities set alongside rivers or the ocean. Age-old traditions in carving, dancing, and mask making have survived through rounds of new cultures bombarding their own, as has the language in most of the region. The subsistence lifestyle, with dependence on hunting and fishing for the main food source, continues as an important way of life, although the people also make good use of modern transportation and technology. *Central Yup'ik* is the main dialect; others are *Norton Sound* and *Egegik*, and in the *Hooper Bay-Chevak* and *Nunivak* dialects, the name for the people and language is *Cup'ik* (CHOO-pik).

This unnamed Savoonga man was 103 years old when his photo was taken with two children in 1939. Savoonga and Gambell are the two communities on the isolated St. Lawrence Island. Subsistence hunters pursue sea mammals and birds as essentials to a traditional diet. *(UAF-1976-43-2, University of Alaska Fairbanks, Alaska and Polar Regions, John Neville Collection)*

Below: Gambell carvers make ingenious figures from walrus ivory and whalebone. *(Tricia Brown)*

Siberian Yupik (sigh-BEER-ee-un YOU-pik). Remote St. Lawrence Island, off the Bering Sea coast, is home to these Native Alaskans who are linked by family history and language to the Siberian Yupik in Russia. Sea mammals, fish, and birds have always been important to the people for food as well as for materials to make boats, clothing, fishing gear, and works of art. The *Siberian Yupik* language is unique among Alaska's Eskimo peoples.

Left: Three men of Nushagak, including the chief, were photographed by Charles O. Farciot in the 1880s. The settlement of Nushagak preexisted present-day Dillingham and was the site of a Russian Orthodox Mission. By 1900, several salmon canneries sprang up nearby. The influenza epidemic of 1918-19 devastated the village, leaving many orphans and leading to the establishment of a hospital and orphanage at Kanakanak. *(ASL-P277-017-009, Alaska State Library, Wickersham State Historic Site Photographs)*

Traditional
Homeland
Iñupiat

The Messenger Feast, or Kivgiq, involved a runner who traveled from the host village to another village to invite them to the dance-feast. The Messenger Stick (Ayauppiaq) would have items attached to it, symbolizing the gifts that the host desired. The Runner (Aqpatat) in this photo from the turn of the last century has labret holes in his lower lip. (ASL-P320-22, *Alaska State Library, Rev. Samuel Spriggs Photographs)*

Iñupiat (in-YOU-pea-at). The people of the Far North, the whaling and sealing people, have lived in the Northwest and Arctic for many thousands of years. They have traditionally relied on sea mammals as well as land animals, such as caribou, for sustenance as well as raw materials for clothing and tools. An individual is termed an Iñupiaq, as is any reference to the culture or language. Many smaller villages are scattered throughout the region, and four larger communities are found on the coast: Nome, Kotzebue, Point Hope, and Barrow. Two main dialects exist in the language: *North Alaskan Iñupiaq* and *Seward Peninsula Iñupiaq.*

Athabascan (ath-uh-BA-scun). Settling along the riverways of the vast Interior and into Southcentral Alaska (and Canada), the Athabascan people, like other Native Alaskans, made wise use of materials from the natural world for their needs. The movement of the various bands within the region, while termed "nomadic," was orderly and seasonal in keeping with the best hunting, trapping, and fishing times. Settlement into more permanent villages occurred with the coming of non-Natives, when the people adopted some of the outsiders' ways. They engaged in trade, allowed their children to be schooled, and many adopted a new religion. There are eleven unique languages (versus dialects) among Alaska's Athabascan people, including *Ahtna, Deg Hit'an, Holikachuk, Koyukon, Upper Kuskokwim, Dena'ina (Tanaina), Tanacross, Tanana, Upper Tanana, Han,* and *Gwich'in.*

Traditional
Homeland
Athabascan

Left: Alice, Maggie, and Elia Laroyen of Tanana donned their traditional winter clothing for an outdoor portrait. *(UAF-897-2, University of Alaska Fairbanks, Alaska and Polar Regions, Mr. and Mrs. Gregory Kokrine Collection)*

17

Eyak (EE-ak). A small group bordered on three sides by other Native cultures, these people have survived with their distinctive identity intact. Their homelands cover the region from Cordova to Yakutat. The waters of Prince William Sound and the Copper River were important natural resources, and the Eyak relied heavily on subsistence fishing, as well as hunting for birds and land mammals. There are no living Native speakers of the *Eyak* language.

Traditional
Homeland
Eyak

Right: A young man's beaded jacket reflects the influence of Athabascan neighbors on clothing in the Eyak area. This early 20th-century photo was taken in the Katalla area, where Eyak people were strongly influenced by the Tlingit, Athabascan, and Sugpiaq (Alutiiq) cultures that bordered them. *(Alaska State Library, Ray W. Moss Photograph Collection)*

Traditional
Homeland
Tlingit

Tlingit (KLINK-it). Few parts of Southeast were *not* in Tlingit control in centuries past, where the people have flourished in this forested region, harvesting the land and sea, carving totems and masks, and weaving intricate robes and baskets. This group offered the greatest resistance to non-Native interlopers, and suffered greatly in retaliation, from Russian and American forces alike. The *Tlingit* language was oppressed for many decades, and other means of cultural expression, such as carving, weaving, and potlatching, were nearly wiped out under dominant outside forces, and has again been restored. Elders and educators are working to keep the language alive.

Above: Three brothers of the Shangukeidi were formally photographed in 1907. From left: Kaalgei, Sx'anduoo, and Swaatk'i (Yindayaank'). *(Alaska State Library, William R. Norton Photographs)*

Haida (HIGH-da). The Kaigani Haida, those who left Canada for Alaska in the late 1700s, paddled north in massive canoes and settled

Traditional
Homeland
Haida

Above: A somber group
gathered in ceremonial
dress at Klinkwan's last
traditional ceremony
before village evacuation
to Hydaburg, circa 1900.
*(ASL-P87-0316, Alaska
State Library, Winter &
Pond Photographs)*

on a portion of Prince of Wales Island, in southern Southeast. The
people had migrated north from Haida Gwaii, the Canadian island
group also known as the Queen Charlotte Islands. The people often
call themselves the *Kiis Haade* and their Native language is *Haida*.
Respected for their incredible carving and weaving skills, the people
remain culturally connected to their relatives in Canada.

Tsimshian (sim-she-AN). The traditional home of the Tsimshian people
is in western British Columbia. However, today's Alaskans are descendants
of a group that crossed the border in 1887 with a non-Native missionary
seeking to establish a model community, now known as Metlakatla, on
Annette Island in Southeast. While many of their traditional ways fell

Traditional
Homeland
Tsimshian

out of practice—such as carving, potlatching, and speaking their Native language—in recent decades, the Alaskans have experienced a cultural revival, drawing inspiration and knowledge from their Canadian cousins and distant past. Their language is called *Tsimshian*.

Tsimshian carver Casper Mather was born in Old Metlakatla, British Columbia, in 1876, and was among those who emigrated to Annette Island with missionary William Duncan. Mather began his carving career at midlife, in the 1930s, and continued until his death in his nineties. *(Alaska State Library, Donald Burrus Photograph Collection)*

A basket woven by contemporary artist Delores Churchill is a museum piece. *(Courtesy Alaska Museum)*

Looking Forward, Looking Back

In the evenings after work in Sitka, a Tlingit woman heads for the beach to collect *gumboots*, or chitons, for her elderly aunt. In Barrow, an Iñupiaq broadcaster spends one afternoon a week at the radio station recording programs in her Native language. On Unalaska Island, a Unanga^x (Aleut) Elder teaches others the art of making bentwood hunting visors. In the Athabascan village of Huslia, a woman speaks her ancestral language, *Koyukon*, in retelling stories she heard from her grandfather long ago. At Ted Stevens International Airport in Anchorage, a Yup'ik woman arrives from Bethel and greets her grown son, who can't wait for Mom to make his favorite dessert: *agutak*, also known as "Eskimo ice cream," made

Facing page: At Tununak, Geraldine Fairbanks shows how herring is woven into a grass "garland" before drying on outdoor racks.
(Roy Corral)

Subsistence fisherman and brothers Moses (left) and Larry Dirks use more modern methods than their ancestors.
(Roy Corral)

with whipped fat and berries. Like 24,000 other Natives living in Anchorage (nearly 8 percent of "Alaska's biggest village" is Native), he feels good when he eats good traditional food.

In Alaska's farthest reaches and in its larges cities, people are carrying on their Native ways. They do so in thousands of variations of the old and new.

They hunt, fish, and gather food to eat, connecting with the land as well as for nutritional and economic necessity. Those who do share with those who can't. Even many with cash wage jobs find time to participate in this lifeline. Schools in many villages start early in fall so they can let out early in spring, when families go fishing.

"Subsistence is truly a way of life, from one season to the next," said Teri Rofkar, a Tlingit woman from Sitka. "It's not something you do separately. It's a part of you. A kind of important part for me."

Rofkar is an expert weaver, known for her basketry and robes. Likewise, many other Alaska Natives carve and weave, making tools, clothing, and artworks in the fashion of those before them. They congregate for feasts to honor the dead and celebrate the living, using ancient words held in the memory for those occasions. They sing old songs and write new ones. Sometimes their drums are still covered the old way with animal gut or skins, but today the heads are as

An Iñupiaq woman from Nuiqsut fishes in the frozen Colville River. *(Thomas Sbampato/ AlaskaStock.com)*

Foreign fur traders spread into the Interior during the 1800s, bringing with them their special brand of music, which was adapted by the local people. Athabascan fiddlers went on to develop their own blend of music, and today Old-Time Fiddling Festivals are a seasonal attraction for musicians and dancers alike. A few Athabascan fiddlers have even recorded their own CDs. *(Matt Hage/ AlaskaStock.com)*

likely to be made of nylon. In a pinch during a visit to Anchorage, a Yup'ik drummer accompanied himself on a plastic Frisbee with an old wooden kitchen spoon, for an impromptu session teaching dance and song to a friend's child.

Alaska Natives are not relics stuck in a time warp of the past. Their cultures are more than shards of pottery or shreds of basketry in museum cases. Alaska Native cultures are alive today in ways expected and unexpected. There are some common themes between culture groups, yet innumerable twists in the way circumstances and cultures combine. But as they have been throughout time, Alaska Natives are innovators, adapting old traditions and creating new ones, linking past with present in a continuum of their cultures. They are today's version of Alaska's original people.

The Beginnings

Alaska's original people occupied the Northland many thousands of years ago. Some Native stories recall the distant past, when people and animals shared the same language and could transform into one

Honored Haida leaders gather for a portrait in this historic image from Old Kasaan. *(ASL-Kasaan-07 Old Kasaan Potlatch, Alaska State Library, Historical Collections.)*

another. In Yup'ik cosmology, beings moved between realms during a time when "the earth was thin."

In more recent times, Alaska's people traveled across the land, along the coasts, and up the rivers. Stone tools found in some early campsites are believed to be 10,000 to 11,000 years old.

Archaeologists believe that North America's first people filtered from the landmass known today as Asia. They traveled in small bands at different times, as they hunted large mammals across the continent-sized land bridge connecting Siberia and Alaska. Ancient sites from this era have been found on the North Slope, in the Interior, in the Aleutian Islands, and in Southeast. The tools found in these places vary, indicating the existence of different cultures at similar times. Perhaps some of the early people boated along the coastlines. Archaeologists offer various scenarios about how these ancient people dispersed throughout Alaska and their relationships to each other and later arrivals.

Language Affinities

The early people included groups broadly defined as Paleoindian, Na-Dene, and Eskaleut by linguists looking at language links and archaeologists looking at tool traditions. A simplistic portrait of their connections to today's Native cultures goes something like this: Paleoindians, who were some of the earliest people, filtered through Alaska in a southerly migration to the lower continent. Later came the Na-Dene Indians, who were ancestors to Alaska's Athabascan, Eyak, and Tlingit people. The Eskaleut slowly filtered in along the coastlines even later, and in their movements developed into Alaska's Unanga^x (Aleut) culture and the Iñupiat, Yup'ik, and Siberian Yupik, as well as, say linguists, the Sugpiaq (Alutiiq). Ancient links to the Haida and Tsimshian Indians are more obscure.

In 2005, Alaska's population of Natives was about 106,000, roughly 16 percent of the statewide population, the highest percentage of Native Americans in any state. However, in 1930, slightly more than half the population was Native. The numbers declined for various reasons, from the devastating effects of tuberculosis on the Native population, to surges in non-Native settlement during and after World War II and the years surrounding the construction of the trans-Alaska pipeline.

Survival Adaptations

Alaska's indigenous people developed ingenious ways to survive off the land and sea, using minerals and plant and animal materials for tools, clothing, and shelter. They were astute observers, reading their environment for clues to weather patterns and animal migrations. Many engaged in long-range trade through aboriginal networks.

Women from Wales, one packing a baby in her parka, are wearing the old-style fur parkas in this century-old photo. Women's parkas were characterized by a hem that was longer in front and back than the sides. *(UAF-1959-875-32, University of Alaska, Fairbanks, Alaska and Polar Regions, S.R. Bernardi Photographs)*

They developed complicated social structures and belief systems to govern individual actions and group activities, with undesirable consequences to those who became careless and offensive. People committed their personal and cultural histories to memory, along with their rules for behaving and living. All this vital information was passed on from generation to generation through examples and stories.

Contact

The year 1741 marked the second voyage of Capt. Vitus Bering into the North Pacific. Exploring for the Russian czar, Bering was the first European to make contact with Alaska Natives.

Prolonged contact with Westerners began at various times for Natives in different regions, from about 1750 along the southern coast through about 1870 in the more inland regions. Explorers, fur traders, gold miners, and missionaries were among the earliest outsiders. They brought different attitudes, values, foods, tools, and customs. Alaska's various Native groups felt all these influences, some of which they willingly embraced; others they did not.

The newcomers inadvertently introduced foreign germs. Disease epidemics raged during the early years of contact with non-Natives, sometimes decimating and reducing Native populations to a fraction of their precontact strength.

The influx of outsiders changed how Natives used the land. Settlements and towns sprang up on traditional hunting, fishing, and ceremonial grounds, and land transactions generally ignored territorial claims by Natives. Tlingits in Southeast tried to regain land as early as 1890, when Chief Johnson of the Taku tribe sued—albeit unsuccessfully—whites who built a dock in Juneau on his property. However, in 1935, the Tlingit–Haida Central Council successfully sued the government for $7.2 million for taking aboriginal lands in 1902 when it formed the forest reserve now known as Tongass National Forest.

Among the early influences that had long-lived effects were missionaries and educational policies. After Russia sold Alaska to the U.S. government in 1867, Alaska Natives fell under the law for a time as "uncivilized tribes." As General Agent of Education, Sheldon Jackson divided Alaska among various religious denominations, which established missions and schools to give the Native children a Christian upbringing and education. Many Native people today attend the same churches as did their parents and grandparents who

St. George residents Agnes and Anna Lekanof wait aboard the Army transport ship SS Delarof en route to Southeast Alaska. Nine Unanga^x (Aleut) villages on six islands were evacuated during June and July 1942. More than 10 percent of the people died during World War II, including many Elders and the very young. The U.S. government offered a formal apology and monetary reparations in 1988. *(UAF-1970-11-94, University of Alaska Fairbanks, Alaska and Polar Regions, San Francisco Call-Bulletin, Aleutian Islands Photographs)*

The village of Chalkyitsik was known as "Fishhook" in 1942, when George Dale and Evelyn Butler photographed this young girl, labeling the photo, "First time school." Not until 1972, with the passage of the Molly Hootch Act, did Native children receive equal treatment in the state's school system. Teenagers in small rural villages had been sent to boarding schools. After 1972, another 205 secondary schools opened, and Alaska Native children were able to attend school in their home villages. *(ASL-P306-0155, Alaska State Library, Evelyn Butler and George Dale Photographs)*

were introduced to Western religions. The missionaries also curtailed many traditional Native ceremonies, practically to extinction in some places. Although some of the earliest missionaries developed written alphabets for Native languages and translated church writings, the missionaries and government teachers who came later insisted that the Native children learn and speak only English in the schools, often punishing them if they forgot. In 1972, a federal law passed requiring bilingual education in many of the schools.

For many years, Natives were treated as second-class citizens, made to attend separate schools and restaurants and to sit in the rear rows of theaters. In 1945, Alaska's territorial legislature finally passed a nondiscrimination act—the nation's first—that required businesses to remove signs banning Native trade.

The 1940s, '50s, and '60s quickened the pace of change. World War II brought the military to Alaska. Many Native men served during the war and afterward found jobs building and maintaining military facilities in rural Alaska. In societies that valued self-reliance and hunting prowess, more men found themselves juggling cash wage employment with subsistence activities. Women likewise were adjusting their roles and activities as they faced changing economic, educational, and religious values. With the proliferation of Western ways, young Natives had a confusing range of role models.

Some individuals denied their Native-ness to function more easily in the dominant society. Others felt anger, shame, and confusion, their futures clouded by cycles of despondency and despair. The long-term erosion of self-identity and self-esteem contributed to high rates of alcoholism and suicide in rural Alaska. These days numerous Native communities are actively involved in sobriety efforts. Some villages prohibit the importation, sale, and use of alcohol, with searches of incoming freight and visitors. The efforts also include sobriety camps and healing ceremonies emphasizing Native spirituality.

Politics

One of the landmarks for Alaska Natives came in 1971 with passage
of the Alaska Native Claims Settlement Act (ANCSA). It was the
climax to many years of political activity by Alaska Natives, and it set
the stage for even more.

In 1912, Tlingit and Haida people had formed the Alaska Native
Brotherhood to win citizenship; at the time, Natives had no rights
under the U.S. government. The ANB and its sister organization,
Alaska Native Sisterhood, still in existence today, were forerunners
of later Native organizations including the Tlingit–Haida Central
Council and the Alaska Federation of Natives.

In 1935, Congress passed legislation allowing Natives to sue the
federal government for land taken by the United States. The Tlingit–
Haida Council was the first to file a claim for lands taken for Tongass
National Forest. In 1958, the Alaska Statehood Act recognized
Native rights to some lands and Native land claims continued
accumulating. Soon the entire state was tied up in litigation, and in

Holy Ascension
Orthodox Church on
Unalaska Island is a
National Historic
Landmark. *(Roy Corral)*

A Sitka black-tailed fawn, just weeks old, with a centuries-old red cedar on eastern Prince of Wales Island, bordering Clarence Strait. *(Robert Spencer Ingman)*

fall 1966 a coalition of Natives formed to push a federal settlement of Native claims through Congress. The new Alaska Federation of Natives found unexpected allies in oil companies, particularly after the North Slope discovery of the Prudhoe Bay field. The AFN claims, supported by the oil companies wanting to settle the issue and proceed with construction of an oil pipeline, resulted in the Alaska Native Claims Settlement Act. It created thirteen regional Native corporations and 205 village corporations to manage an endowment of $1 billion and 44 million acres.

The original act made no provision to extend corporation shares to Native children born after ANCSA's passage and allowed non-Natives to eventually buy into the corporations; amendments to change these provisions were later passed. ANSCA corporations were mandated to return profits to their shareholders, which has often been achieved by harvesting timber or extracting minerals, sometimes conflicting with more traditional Native land uses.

ANCSA also had an unexpected outcome, triggering a resurgence of tribal claims of sovereignty in Alaska, noted Will Mayo, former president of the Tanana Chiefs Conference, Inc. "The bill was badly written in terms of preserving and continuing the existence of Native people as an identifiable land group," he said. "The corporations exist, and many Native people are deeply involved in them and have benefited. So they are a part of who we are. Nevertheless, more and more villages have transferred village corporation lands to tribal governments. . . . Tribal governments are asserting more rights. The question before the courts is: Do Alaska tribes have powers of other tribes in the nation?"

Tribal status has specific meaning under federal law for Native self-government. This includes giving tribal governments control of such things as adoptions and foster placement of Native children, handling misdemeanor cases through tribal courts, and in some cases levying taxes and managing wildlife on tribal lands. Tribal governments in Alaska have achieved some of these powers, but not all.

At issue is whether tribal powers in Alaska will extend to fish and game management. In the last decades of the 20th century, subsistence became one of the most heated political issues in Alaska. Currently Natives have priority for subsistence over commercial and sport uses on federal lands through a "rural preference" in the 1981 Alaska National Interest Lands Conservation Act (ANILCA). The courts are deadlocked over the matter of whether this priority extends to state lands. Many Native leaders worry that Congress will someday amend ANILCA to remove this protection. Some of them see tribal powers as a way to maintain Native priorities to fish and game.

Young Jerrald John discovers bear tracks along the Chandalar River, north of Arctic Village. (Roy Corral)

Subsistence is "an important part of the larger historical question about the status rights and future survival of Alaska's aboriginal peoples," according to a 1994 report from the Alaska Natives Commission. "The economics of most Native villages in Alaska remain underdeveloped, artificial dependencies of government where few jobs and relatively small amounts of cash exist. Without a secure protein base of wild renewable fish and game resources, the poorest and most traditional villagers are doomed to economic and social deterioration. . . . In addition to supplying food and other necessities, (subsistence) provides people with productive labor, personal self

A spring 2001 whale hunt ends in success for Eugene Brower's whaling crew in Barrow. With the aid of block-and-tackle, crewmembers haul it onto the ice. *(Roy Corral)*

Facing page: Tlingit carver Nathan Jackson at his studio in Saxman. *(Roy Corral)*

esteem, strong family and community relationships, and a cultural foundation that can never be replaced or duplicated by any other arrangement."

United But Separate

Outside the political arena, some of the most visible aspects of Alaska's diverse Native cultures are seen today in expressions of dance and arts.

There is no mistaking Yup'ik dancers with their dance fans and *kuspuks,* Tlingit dancers in button robes and Chilkat weavings, or Athabascans in beaded moosehide regalia. Subtle variations in items such as dance fans, headdress, and style and trim of robes, *kuspuks,* and parkas identify specific villages, clans, or regions within each culture.

The Killer Whale Clan dances at the Four Clans longhouse in Southeast. *(Roy Corral)*

Traditional expressions of Native art also vary between many of the cultures. Athabascans are noted for birch-bark baskets, beading and porcupine-quill embroidery, and skin-sewing. Distinctive to the Unangaˆx (Aleut) culture are finely woven grass baskets. Ivory scrimshaw, baleen basketry, and fur- and skin-sewing are some of the better known Iñupiat arts. The Southeast Indian groups produced master woodworkers, men who carved giant totem poles, houseposts, and canoes and who were skilled in steaming and bending wood to make boxes of all sizes and descriptions. The women wove spruce-root and cedar-bark baskets and ceremonial robes from bark, wool, and furs. Some Native artists today draw upon their cultural heritage in producing contemporary works, while others focus on more traditional designs and techniques.

Language is another area of cultural distinction. Even within a single language, numerous dialects may still be heard. But across the cultures, people have passed on their histories and rules for living through stories of one form or another. Children were warned against bad behaviors through cautionary tales. Other stories told about animals and people. The Raven, with dual personalities as creator and trickster, appears as a central character in many stories from different groups.

Although oral narratives are no longer the primary method of information transmission, linguists and Native speakers have done considerable work in documenting languages and stories. Most of this work has been supported or conducted by the Alaska Native Language Center, which opened in 1972 and is the nation's leading research center on Alaska's aboriginal languages.

Every culture worldwide celebrates with food, and so it is with Alaska Native people. This spans everything from the simple act of providing Elders with fresh salmon, to the sharing by Iñupiat whalers of each bowhead landed, to the ceremonial distribution of a Yup'ik boy's first seal, to potlatches with dancing to celebrate Tlingit totem raisings.

Haida silversmiths are renowned for their craftsmanship.
(Roy Corral)

Tsimshian parents Jack
and Iris Huckleberry pose
with year-old Jacklynn.
(Roy Corral)

Cultural Revitalization

Many things occurring among Native Alaskans today fall into the
category of "cultural revitalization." This includes the establishment
of cultural centers and museums in places such as Bethel, Kodiak,
Kotzebue, Unalaska, Ketchikan, Barrow, and Akutan. These centers
serve as repositories for cultural artifacts and offer central meeting
places for communities.

A federal repatriation act has made way for the return of many
human remains and ceremonial objects, most of which were taken in
archaeological excavations and ethnographic collecting trips in the
early 1900s and housed in museums outside of Alaska. In addition,
archaeologists handling new excavations consult with Elders and
work closely with Natives in the communities to ensure appropriate
handling of the materials.

Cultural camps, where Elders share traditional knowledge, are a
popular way for Native people to reconnect with their heritage. There
are also the numerous language and oral history projects in schools

and communities. Efforts are underway throughout Alaska by various organizations to document Native place-names and stories that go with them. In addition, dance festivals and other events such as totem raisings, give Alaska Natives various opportunities to celebrate their cultures in meaningful ways, as well as revive ceremonies that fell into disuse.

A cooperative effort by the Alaska Federation of Natives, University of Alaska, and the National Science Foundation calls for integrating traditional Native knowledge into the state's Rural Systemic Initiative. This has among its many goals to strengthen Alaska Native self-identity and to recognize the contributions of Native people, to integrate Native ways of knowledge and teaching into the curriculum, and to improve Alaska Native students academic performance in science.

Clearly, Native cultures in Alaska have undergone many changes in a relatively short period of time. Yet they are enduring, with the resilience of ever-adapting people.

A party of young hunters use binoculars and scopes to scan the Chandalar Valley, looking for moose to sustain the family for the next year. *(Roy Corral)*

Unangaˆx (Aleut)

Traditional
Homeland
Unangaˆx

The people known as Aleut call themselves Unangaˆx (*oo-NUNG-uh*) and claim the volcanic, windswept arc of southwest Alaska along what geologists call the "Ring of Fire." Their homelands stretch about a thousand miles through the ocean from the lower third of the Alaska Peninsula to the far western tip of the Aleutian Islands, including the more northerly Pribilof Islands.

During the 2000 census, about 2,300 Unangaˆx were living in the region's villages—Adak, Atka, Nikolski, Akutan, Belkofski, Cold Bay, Unalaska, False Pass, Nelson Lagoon, King Cove, Sand Point, St. Paul, and St. George. Attu Island, once occupied by ancestors of today's people, is now a Coast Guard LORAN Station. Unga and Pauloff Harbor likewise are no longer occupied. And almost as many Unangaˆx live elsewhere in Alaska as those who still occupy their home territory.

Like other Alaska Natives today, Unangaˆx are mobile members of modern society, pursuing jobs, education, and other opportunities wherever they lead. Yet cultural practices—fishing, seal hunting,

Facing page: Master weaver Sharon Kay returned to her childhood home in 2007. Beyond her is the house where Kay's grandmother, Cecilia Foster (1894-1967), raised nine children; she spent her entire life on Unga Island. *(Sharon Kay)*

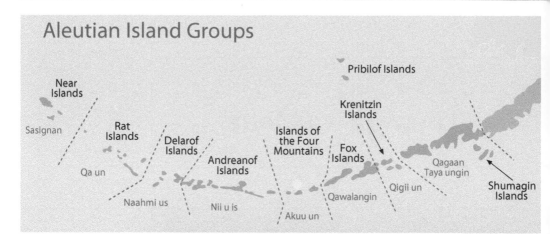

Aleutian Island Groups

Near Islands

Pribilof Islands

Rat Islands

Krenitzin Islands

Sasignan

Delarof Islands

Islands of the Four Mountains

Fox Islands

Andreanof Islands

Qagaan Taya ungin

Qa un

Qigii un

Shumagin Islands

Naahmi us

Nii u is

Qawalangin

Akuu un

Pat Lekanoff-Gregory models a brand-new bentwood visor crafted in the same way her ancestors have made them for centuries. *(Roy Corral)*

gathering beach foods—remain important, particularly for those who depend on subsistence foods.

"You know, we say, 'When the tide is out, the table is set,'" said Patricia Lekanoff-Gregory, of Unalaska. "We're always getting gumboots [chitons] and sea eggs [urchins] for the Elders. You can eat the sea eggs raw, just cut them in half and scoop out the roe." Gumboots are eaten raw or slightly steamed, dipped in butter and garlic, she said. "You just click one off the rock, cut off the bony part in back and eat the tongue. They're real chewy, but have a good taste."

In some Unanga^x communities, particularly those of the Alaska Peninsula, people make their living fishing for salmon commercially. Several communities host huge fishing ports and international seafood processing plants to serve Bering Sea pollock and cod trawlers. Relatively few Unanga^x participate directly in these fisheries, although some village corporations are involved in the shore-based fishery developments or share in Bering Sea bottomfish harvests through community development quotas.

Today's waterborne commerce is a modern version of what has been going on in this part of the world for centuries. The early people traveled and traded extensively in their region and beyond. This watery thoroughfare also brought Unanga^x

"You know, we say, 'When the tide is out, the table is set. . . '"

Unanga^x leader Larry Merculieff above a beach full of seals on St. Paul Island. The city of St. Paul is visible in the distance. *(Roy Corral)*

Unangaˆx (Aleut) dancers traveled from Atka to participate in the 1996 conference of the Alaska Federation of Natives. *(Roy Corral)*

(Aleuts) the earliest and harshest contact with outsiders of any of Alaska Native people.

Russian fur traders sailed to the Aleutian Islands in the mid-1700s to exploit the region's abundance of sea otters. They found an estimated 12,000 to 15,000 indigenous people in seasonal camps and villages, who formed about eight tribes by island groups. The Russians called them "Aleut," a Siberian term they also used for the more easterly Sugpiaq (Alutiiq), coastal people with similar lifestyles but a different language and the traditional enemy of the Unangaˆx.

The Russians marveled at the people's seafaring skills in their lightweight, skin-covered kayaks; they knew fur-trading success depended on Unangaˆx hunters. Native resistance was fierce, but the gun-wielding Russians exerted control and settled. Traders took Unangaˆx men on months-long sea otter hunts as far away as

California and Hawaii. The remaining villagers suffered without their hunters and became more dependent on the Russians for food and clothing. Absence of the Unangaˆx men also disrupted the passing on of ceremonies, dancing, and storytelling. The people were further decimated by infectious disease epidemics. Within a half-century of Russian occupation, only about 2,500 Unangaˆx remained.

Elements of Russian influence are still evident among Unangaˆx people. Russian surnames today are a legacy of long-ago marriages between traders and Native women. Similarly the Russian Orthodox religion—introduced with a mission to Alaska in 1841—still has a devoted following. The saintly priest Ivan Veniaminov, sympathetic to Aleut culture, worked with Unangaˆx scholars to develop a written alphabet, taught people to read their language, and conducted services in it.

Today *Unangam Tunuu*, the Unangaˆx language, is spoken by Elders and middle-aged adults, used in special church services, and taught in schools. In Atka, one of the most traditional villages, children still speak the language at home. Two dialects of *Unangam Tunuu* remain—Western, spoken on Atka, and Eastern, spoken elsewhere. A renewed interest in language and storytelling, a revival of Unangaˆx dance, and efforts by communities such as Unalaska and Akutan to establish cultural centers and museums reflect an increasing interest in the heritage of Unangaˆx.

The early Unangaˆx were masters of their treeless maritime environment, using driftwood, rocks, grasses, fish skins, animal bones, and bird feathers for tools, shelter, and clothing. The women painstakingly wove grass for many uses—sleeping mats, socks, and vessels tight enough to hold water. Unangaˆx baskets woven today, still commonly known as Aleut baskets, are finely made and command premium prices.

Unangaˆx men were renowned for their boat-making skills, their signature craft being the *iqyax*, skin-covered kayaklike craft. Today, the art of *iqyax*-building has reemerged as a cultural connection. In the mid-1990s, high school students in Unalaska completed two of

Unangaˆx man in raingear and visor.
(Clark James Mishler/ AlaskaStock.com)

An Atka Island dancer prepares to perform at an Alaskan Federation of Natives Convention. *(Roy Corral)*

Facing page: Unalaska Church of the Holy Ascension of Christ Church faces east, as Russian Orthodox tradition prescribes. *(Roy Corral)*

these boats; one, a wide-bodied *iqyax* for fishing or carrying cargo; the other of classic split-bow design, built narrow and long for speed. After practicing in the high school's Olympic-sized pool, they paddled in the village lake and Unalaska Bay. The Unangan youngsters displayed almost immediate proficiency with the boats, said Patricia Lekanoff-Gregory, almost as if they were born into it.

Today Russian Orthodox churches throughout the region are undergoing restoration, partly with federal funds received in 1989 as belated settlement for treatment of the Aleuts during World War II. The war brought Allied military occupation, Japanese invasion, and nearly a year of air, sea, and ground combat. Attu villages were captured by the enemy; the U.S. government transported most other Unangaˆx (Aleuts) to desolate internment camps in Southeast, where one of every ten people died. Reparation funds were used in a massive restoration of Unalaska's historic Church of the Holy Ascension of Christ, once considered one of the nation's twelve most endangered historic landmarks.

Riding Ungikan Home

By Barbara Švarný Carlson

Thomas Wolfe said, "You can't go home again." Having lived for many years away from my "village" of Unalaska in the Aleutian Islands, I find that a disturbing thought. For me, Ungiikan, the old stories of the Unangaˆx, Aleutian Aleuts, are the ticket for a metaphorical return trip. As I study and learn more about the stories, I learn more about what it means to be Unangaˆx.

Growing up in Unalaska in the 1950s and '60s with three younger sisters, I learned as much as anyone was learning about our culture. We were raised rich by relatives who lived nearby or visited often. Our mother, Gertrude Hope Švarný—of Unangaˆx, English, and possibly Russian heritage—had lived most of her life in Unalaska. Our father, Samuel Švarný, of Slovakian heritage, had been in Unalaska three years. They spent time taking us special places outdoors, teaching us many uses for Native foods. We developed an appreciation for udaˆx (dry fish), chaduˆx (seal oil), lustuˆx (pickled sea lion flipper), and qungaayuˆx (the hump from a humpback salmon). We learned never to harvest more than we could use or share.

There were things, however, that we did not learn, such as the old stories, our language, and the name by which our ancestors had called themselves. We did not know that we were Unangaˆx nor that we were one of the Qawalangin Tribe of Unalaska. The name "Aleut" was used by the Russians as they moved from Atuˆx (Attu Island) eastward through Alaska during the 18th century. The term "Aleut" was eventually adopted by their people, contributing to the erosion of our indigenous culture.

Left: This circa-1880 photo from St. Paul demonstrates the influence of non-Natives on the Unangaˆx (Aleut) population after a century of contact with outsiders.
(ASL-PCA-185, Alaska State Library, Gray and Hereford Photograph Collection)

Published in 1826, these sketches depict Unangaˆx (Aleut) men in two styles of baidarka, or skin boat. The drawings appeared in Atlas of the Northern Part of the Pacific Ocean, which the Russian Imperial Navy Department compiled in sheets from reports and maps by Gavriil Andreevich Sarychev. Empress Catherine II sponsored the expedition from 1785–94 in which Sarychev described and mapped many of the Aleutian Islands. (ASL-P20-056 , Alaska State Library, Alaska Purchase Centennial Collection)

Below: Russian Orthodox cemetery and chapel on Aleutians. (Dan Parrett/ AlaskaStock.com)

Though proud to be Aleut, I began to realize that many other Alaska Native people appeared to know more about their heritage. In the 1970s, I was privileged to assist the Alaska Native Heritage Festival at the Anchorage Museum of History and Art. The dynamic Native orators at this festival often gave their names of self-designation—Iñupiat instead of the Eskimo, Tsimshian instead of Indian. I wondered if we Aleuts had ever called ourselves something else. Mom said she learned we were Unangaˆx. This sent me searching to learn more.

Storytelling emerged as an important link to my Unangaˆx culture when I became a parent. My children needed to know about their heritage. They needed to hear the old stories, the Ungiikan. They needed to see people living the culture, dancing, and telling stories, to have these

things to teach their children. But I had been told for years that our language was gone and that hardly anyone had heard the old stories. Then I received *Stories Out of Slumber* (1979), a book of Ungiikan rewritten by Unalaska teacher Ray Hudson. His sensitivity helped me brave the ethnocentric bias present in much of the literature, to sift through misinformation, and try to find the truth.

While grateful that information was available, I also felt embarrassed and disconcerted to have to depend on writing by our conquerors and other non-Unangaˆx. Why could I not learn anything from my own people? The Unangaˆx had survived by integrating with the dominant cultures, first Russian, then American. Many traditional ways, including telling the old stories, fell into disuse as our people mastered new cultural and language skills. Despite this, not all was forgotten. Some Elders have courageously decided to discuss the old ways.

The work of scholars helps me know what questions to ask. What grounds my work, however, is to ask the tradition-keepers whether certain things are true or not. It would be easier if I spoke *Unangan Tunuu*. My eldest son and I studied for a semester and with Unangaˆx linguist Moses Dirks at Alaska Pacific University, but fluency would require much more time and work. Consequently, rather than learning stories from the Elders, I rely on the definitive *Unangam Ungiikangin kayux Tunusangin* (*Aleut Tales and Narratives*), collected in 1909–1910 by Waldamar Jochelson and edited by Knut Bergsland and Dirks (1990). Next, I try to find clues from words and phrases in the language and anthropological texts to discern the context in which a story was originally told. Finally, I take what I've learned back to "the village" and ask questions.

Nick Galaktionoff, an old friend of my father's from Unalaska, has been especially helpful. On more than one occasion, my dad told him to talk to me

Aleut baskets are prized for their exquisite, fine weaving. *(Roy Corral)*

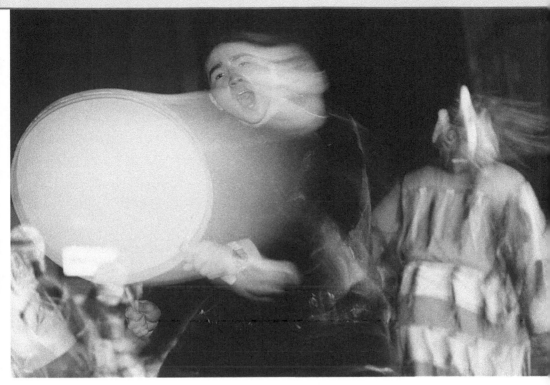

because I study the old stories. As our friendship grew, Nick and I began to work together informally as a master and apprentice.

The Unanga^x way of life was taught and perpetuated through oral tradition, in which important information was committed to memory and passed on by countless generations through the stories. This oral tradition include *Ungiikan*, or stories from the time long ago when things were very different;

Kadaangaadan, narrative stories from more recent times that frequently include names of actual people and places; and *Tunusan*, accounts of life exactly as it happened or could have happened. This oral tradition formed the framework of our Unanga^x education system.

Oral tradition is a different way of learning, because it depends on memory. I was driven to learn new and difficult things to train my mind,

Dancers and drummers in traditional dress perform for the public during the annual Quyana Alaska celebration.
(Roy Corral)

such as doing crossword puzzles, decoding cryptograms, and learning to read music to play piano. Nick was educated in the traditional Unanga^x way among Elders, and he has an exceptional memory. He was incredulous when, as we began to discuss something he had told me, I scurried back to check my

51

A dancer performs at Quyana Alaska, a multicultural celebration held annually during the Alaska Federation of Natives Convention. *(Roy Corral)*

middle, and ending—before telling it. When storytellers achieved mastery, and only then, they stepped inside the role of teacher. To do otherwise could corrupt the lessons that were the intent of the stories.

Today, we are at a critical time in our culture: there are Elders still alive who know some of these stories and can discuss their meanings. If I tell the stories now, even though I am still learning, they can give me advice and my children can hear the stories as children. Fortunately, more people are telling the stories now than a few years ago.

Through Ungiikan, we learn that some of the same ethics we now value, the traditional Unangaˆx valued; that some of the same things we consider sacred, the traditional Unangaˆx considered sacred; that some of what we fear was also feared by the traditional Unangaˆx.

One can be Unangaˆx anywhere, but people in the

notes. Try as I may, my brain seems rigid to function by memory alone. I need my books, paper, and computers. Nick needs only his natural faculties.

In traditional Unangaˆx education, a person might hear a story fifty times during his or her lifetime, learning a little more each time about the right way to live. Likewise good storytellers could read their audiences and know what people might need to hear or have emphasized. The integrity of this oral tradition was protected by protocol. One rule was to know all of the story—beginning, villages are living closest to the heart of tradition. Not only do they live on the land of our ancestors, under the same skies, using the same resources, but their daily activities carry the memories of those who lived before. I've often heard people of my mother's generation lament that they wish they knew more, and then proceed to share precious memories. Eyes light up, someone else enters the conversation, and people begin to mentally revitalize their pasts as they collaborate. Some of what is true about our people remains embedded in the culture today, almost too close to be seen by those closest to it.

As I walk around the lake near where I live in the big city, I watch the colors change through the year and the ways ice crystals form around rocks in creeks before the water freezes over; but I think about Unangaˆx in the villages.

I think about words, phrases, and concepts from Ungiikan, such as knowing we call the sun's afterglow ˆxaniˆgilix; that we know Orion's Belt as "Three Large Men Looking Down;" that we share precious closeness with our lands, skies, and waters; and that *Tutada*, the instruction to "listen," is a crucial, lifelong lesson. I envision the plants, rocks, and animals of those places, and arrange my landscape here to resemble Unalaska as I think about our stories. It takes me home.

Wearing jewelry made by her mother, artist Gertrude Švarný, and a dress of her own design, Barbara recounted the Unangan story called *Achxayachaning* in 1991. (Susanne Swibold)

Barbara Švarný Carlson *lives in Anchorage with her husband, Michael. She is the mother of two sons, Mischa, a graduate of Princeton, and Erik, who hold a doctoral degree from the University of Southern California. In recent years, Barbara consciously decided to set aside storytelling to embrace the work of wildlife and habitat conservation. As president and executive director of Friends of the Anchorage Coastal Wildlife Refuge (FAR) she wrote and helps facilitate the nonprofit group's surveys for sandhill cranes, snow geese, and the Cook Inlet beluga, which has been listed as an Endangered Species. Her mother, Gertrude Švarný, is well-known for her basketry and sculptures of ivory, bone, baleen, and stone, as well as oils and watercolors.*

Sugpiaq (Alutiiq)

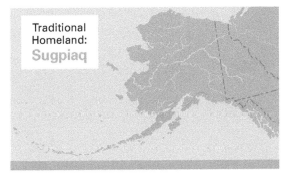

Traditional
Homeland:
Sugpiaq

Just as the Unanga^x were called "Aleut" by Russian overseers, the people in this region were likewise renamed by people outside the culture. Among the names is the term "Alutiiq," which is still commonly used, however many prefer the name the people gave themselves: *Sugpiaq*, which means "genuine" or "real person."

Celebrating "Alutiiq Days" on Kodiak Island, Akhiok villagers gathered around Elder Larry Matfay. He positioned an arrow across the bow as he explained the game of *howaq*. He spoke about how this bow-and-arrow game tested hunters' skill at piercing kelp bulbs, and how the bulbs presented a target similar to that of a sea otter head bobbing in the water. Matfay remembered playing *howaq* as a child, but the game died out when villagers stopped hunting sea otters early in this century. But *howaq* was about to make a comeback, thanks to Matfay and other Elders who share with people anxious to learn more about their Sugpiaq traditions.

Similar reawakenings are going on throughout Alaska's Sugpiaq region. In the city of Kodiak, the Alutiiq Museum opened as one of

Similar reawakenings are going on throughout Alaska's Sugpiaq region.

Facing page: A child in Sugpiaq regalia prepares for a dance at Akhiok. *(Sven Haakanson)*

The ancient Sugpiaq (Alutiiq) were expert seafarers, traveling long distances via skin boats. Here, Alfred Naumoff displays a frame for a model kayak. The full-sized vessel might have one, two, or three holes for paddlers or to carry a passenger. Behind him are paintings of early Unangaˆx and Sugpiaq people, based on illustrations by artists who accompanied early explorers to the region. (Sven Haakanson)

few Native-owned and -operated museums in the nation. Elsewhere in the region, the Nuuciq Spirit Camp is thriving on 800-acre Nuchek Island in Prince William Sound. This cultural retreat, sponsored by Chugach Alaska Corporation, brings Elders and youth together at the site of an ancient Sugpiaq village and important trading center. Chugach Alaska offers this history on Nuchek Island: "At one time, this area was claimed by many nations. The Russians claimed this area by burying a bronze plate with a double-headed eagle. The Spaniards claimed this area by erecting a large cross. The English buried a wine bottle with coins and the Americans hosted a flag. Now Nuchek is owned and controlled by the original landlords."

Spirit camp activities include everything from blazing trails and storytelling to filleting salmon and braiding seal gut. Perhaps as much as anything, spirit camps give people a reprieve from the demands of modern life, allowing young and old to reconnect with the basics of personal, community, and cultural survival.

"Nuuciq Spirit Camp has brought a lot of pride back to the Elders," said Larry Evanoff of Chenega Bay. "You can see it in their face out there, it just livens them up. Makes them feel good to see someone wanting to participate, wanting to learn what they know." A decorated Army veteran, Evanoff is active on the boards of several Native organizations, locally and statewide.

Special cultural celebrations and spirit camps aside, the Sugpiaq people today, particularly those still living in the coastal villages, share in the rich, seafaring heritage of their ancestors.

Ancient village sites dating back 7,000 years on Kodiak Island and the Alaska Peninsula reveal that Sugpiaq ancestors were accomplished maritime hunters and fishermen. They plied the depths for cod and halibut. Using darts and harpoons to hunt sea lions, seals, sea otters, and whales, they paddled after their prey. They took seabirds, such as puffins, and climbed cliffs to gather gull eggs. Seal meat and oil fed them, the oil also fueled their lamps; they used driftwood, sod, thatch, bones, skins, and feathers to make their homes, tools, boats, and clothing.

Many Sugpiaq villagers today remain closely attached to the sea, fishing, and living along Alaska's southcentral and southwestern coasts. Sea oil is still a basic food, used as a dressing or dip for dried fish or roe on kelp, or to mix with berries. In some Sugpiaq villages, land mammals such as bear and caribou are important to the subsistence cycle.

Living along the ocean and waterways of Alaska's southern coast, the Sugpiaq people have long relied on creatures of the seas and tidal zones to sustain them. Fishing remains an important part of the culture. *(Sven Haakanson)*

Chenega Bay's Russian Orthodox church was one of the first buildings constructed in 1984, when villagers chose to relocate the village on Evans Island. The original village was on the southern tip of Chenega Island until it was destroyed by tsunamis following the 1964 earthquake. More than half of its population died. Twenty years later, in 1984, the Sugpiaq village was reborn on Evans Island, where residents today practice a subsistence lifestyle and fish commercially. In 2010, about seventy-five people called Chenega Bay home. *(Courtesy Chenega Corp. and DCRA)*

The Sugpiaq made ingenious adaptations to their environments. Today that is still the case. Fishermen equip their boats with the latest affordable gadgetry, from the electric depth finders to water-cooled holds to keep their catch fresh. The villages are modernized with frame homes, electricity, grocery stores, computers, satellite television, four-wheelers, and daily airplane connections to larger towns. The early Sugpiaq also adopted elements of Unangaˆx (Aleut), Yup'ik, and Tlingit cultures. Those from Prince William Sound used adzed planks and logs along with sod to construct large buildings hinting at Tlingit plank construction. The more common early Sugpiaq dwellings were semi-subterranean sod houses reinforced by whalebones or driftwood, also found in Unangaˆx and Yup'ik country. A spruce-root basket recovered from an ancient Kodiak Island site shows environmental adaptations similar to the Tlingit, who also wove spruce roots. Like the Unangaˆx and Yup'ik, the Sugpiaq depended on skin-covered kayaks and the larger, open skin boats called *angyaqs*.

Sugpiaq (Alutiiq) territory covers the upper Alaska Peninsula from Port Moller to Egegik on the north and from Kupreanoff Point to the Kamishak Bay on the south; it includes Kodiak Island, parts of lower Cook Inlet and Prince William Sound. Sugpiaq villages today include Old Harbor, Akhiok, Karluk, Port Lions, Larsen Bay, and Ouzinkie on Kodiak Island, and Tatitlek and Chenega Bay in Prince William Sound; Cordova hosts one of the largest groups of Sugpiaq in the Sound. Natives of Sugpiaq descent also live in Alaska Peninsula villages such as Chignik and Port Heiden. People throughout the region, however, may still describe themselves to outsiders as Aleut. The Russians applied the name "Aleut" liberally when identifying Natives they encountered, although they further designated the Kodiak Islanders as Koniag and those in Prince William Sound as Chugach. The Native language, *Sugt'stun*, is part of the Aleut-Eskimo linguistic family and is closely related to Yup'ik. About 400 of the estimated 4,000 Sugpiaq (Alutiiq) people still speak some of the language today; about 200 are fluent.

The examination of Sugpiaq identity, as discussed by Gordon Pullar on page 64, is of growing importance to the people as they define their culture in context of contemporary society. Pullar and other leaders orchestrated Sugpiaq conferences in 1997 and 1998 to talk about this issue among others, resulting in a major museum exhibit of Sugpiaq (Alutiiq) artifacts taken from Alaska in the late 1800s and now held by the Smithsonian Institution. Curated by Aron Crowell of the Smithsonian Institution's Arctic

An Alutiq child is engrossed by the beauty of a flower bud. *(Roy Corral)*

Like men in villages all across Alaska, Ephraim Agnot Jr. of Akiok is a fisherman, carpenter, and jack-of-all-trades. *(Roy Corral)*

Facing page: The village of Chignik. The three Chigniks—Chinik Lake, Chignik Lagoon, and the village of Chignik—are mere miles apart on the Alaska Peninsula, but none is accessible by road. Chignik means "big wind." *(Elizabeth Manfred/DCRA)*

Studies Center in Anchorage, the 2001 exhibit was titled "Looking Both Ways: Heritage and Identity of the Alutiiq People." The University of Alaska Press published an exhibit catalog of the same name in 2001, and the Arctic Studies Center created an online version of the exhibit.

The ambitious undertaking included an interactive exhibit so visitors could hear Alutiiq people talking about modern food-gathering and fishing, or Elders talking about how items were made and used, as well as telling stories in their own language. Students in

About 800 petroglyphs and other stone carvings have been found on Kodiak Island, messages in stone from ancestors of today's people. The Alutiiq Museum is working to identify and protect the petroglyphs. *(Sven Haakanson)*

Tatitlek helped to develop the exhibit by interviewing elders in their village for history's information and stories.

In researching the exhibit, Crowell included videotapes of four master skin-sewers from the Sugpiaq, Iñupiat, and Yup'ik regions discussing a 100-year-old squirrel-skin parka at the Smithsonian. The women noted that the maker had used her raw materials fully—the noses of the squirrels remained on the pelts—and had taken extreme care in sewing. The parka showed Sugpiaq and Yup'ik designs.

"It was an everyday hunting parka but it was equally as beautiful as a festive parka," recalled Kodiak's skin-sewer Susan Malutin. She planned to make a replica using about sixty squirrel pelts. "To think that someone that far back took that much time in far more primitive conditions. . . . There was such a culture here, and on an everyday basis they wore these things."

A Sugpiaq (Alutiiq) dancer joins the cultural event called "Celebration," held biennially in Southeast Alaska. *(Christopher Mertl)*

Who Are We, Anyway?

By Gordon L. Pullar

The angry reaction was swift, just as I'd feared. The Native woman in the audience loudly objected at the first mention of the word "Eskimo."

It was 1985, and the anthropologist Dick Jordan was giving a presentation in Kodiak about an archaeo-logical project on the island. This was his second summer working on the project, and he was confused and distressed by the Native people's insistence that they were Aleuts. Their language, after all, was Eskimoan, very close to Yup'ik. He said he would diplomatically explain to the Native people in the audience that they were Eskimos, not Aleuts.

Most people had heard this before and resented it. In their lifetimes they had always been "Aleut" or in their own language, "Alutiiq." Some of the elders remembered referring to themselves as *Sugpiaq*, meaning "a genuine human being," (plural *Sugpiat*) but few were using that term anymore. Of one thing they were certain: they were not Eskimos.

Kodiak's Native people have gone through a number of changes since first contact with the

Pullar leads a group on a tour of Woody Island, known as Tangirnaq to the Sugpiaq (Alutiiq) people. Arrival of Russian fur traders in 1784 changed their lives forever, as they were forced to hunt and gather food for the foreigners. Epidemics killed thousands throughout the region, especially from smallpox, measles, and influenza. Some scholars estimate that the smallpox epidemic of 1835 to 1840 killed two-thirds of the Natives in southern and western Alaska. Afterward, survivors in thirty-plus villages in the Kodiak archipelago gathered into seven communities, including one on Woody Island. Today, while it is unoccupied, Tangirnaq remains an important cultural site. *(Sven Haakanson)*

Russians in 1763, and events and conditions since that time have profoundly impacted who people feel they are.

After nearly 8,000 years of cultural survival, the indigenous people of Kodiak Island came under the rule of outside forces when the first permanent Russian settlement was established there in 1784. Since then, the culture and identity of the people had been under pressure. On August 13, 1784, Russian merchant Gregorii Shelikhov, with two ships armed with cannons, launched a decisive attack against the people of Kodiak Island. Casualties were severe. As many as 2,000 Sugpiat sought protection on a refuge rock, a small island with cliffs that dropped sharply to the sea. Many hundreds perished as the Russians shelled the small island with cannon fire and stormed it with armed men.

The attack was the first in a series of events that traumatized the Sugpiat and confused their identity. These included severe disease epidemics such as the smallpox epidemic of 1837 to 1840, which killed so many people that Russian administrators consolidated Kodiak Island's sixty-five villages into only seven. Others were natural disasters that destroyed villages and forced survivors to relocate. These included the devastating 1912 eruption of Mount Novarupta near the Sugpiaq village of Katmai that destroyed villages on the Alaska Peninsula, and the great earthquake and tsunami of 1964, that destroyed villages on Kodiak Island and in Prince William Sound.

In the summer of 1995, I took my ten-year-old son, Gordon Jr. (Gordy) to visit friends in the Kodiak Island village of Old Harbor (Nuniaq). Although born in Kodiak, my son had lived in Anchorage since he was five and has therefore

In September 2007, Sven Haakanson, Jr., of Old Harbor was named one of twenty-four MacArthur Fellows, a prestigious award recognizing intellectual achievement. Haakanson, who holds a Ph.D. in anthropology from Harvard, is also a mask maker and photographer, and serves as executive director of the Alutiiq Museum in Kodiak. In making the award, the John D. and Catherine T. MacArthur Foundation called Haakanson "the driving force behind the revitalization of indigenous language, culture and customs in an isolated region of North America." *(Roy Corral)*

perhaps developed a different sense of identity than he might have developed that he still resided in Kodiak. He was excited about the visit to Kodiak Village and was anxious to meet other "Aleut" children. He quickly made friends with the boy his age and asked him, "Are you an Aleut?" "No I'm not an Aleut," the boy quickly responded, somewhat indignantly. "I'm a Native!"

This interchange is symbolic in a way, of the issue of identity on Kodiak Island. In another village a few years before a woman who'd lived in the village her entire life asked me in frustration, "Who are we anyway? Are we Aleuts, Alutiiqs, or Eskimos?" She said she felt embarrassed that anthropologists are claiming we were Eskimos and seemingly had proof to support their claim.

Russian occupation on Kodiak Island (1784 to 1867) significantly influenced the way the island's Native people see themselves. Clothing, foods, language, surnames, and, most importantly, the Russian Orthodox religion are the most noticeable. By the time of the 1867 American takeover, most Sugpiat were bilingual, speaking both Sugt'stun and Russian.

When the American education system was introduced in the late 19th century, these bilingual children were not allowed to speak either of the languages they were fluent in and were forced to speak English.

Making matters worse was the existence of a social class of people called "Creoles," that had been created by the Russian–American Co. One way to be a Creole was to have mixed Russian–Native parentage. Another was to be educated in Russia and have returned in a management position for the company. As the Creole classification had no meaning to the newly arrived Americans, many people with that designation came to refer to themselves as Russians in order to get better treatment from the Americans. The Creole

Phyllis Peterson's surname offers clues about Scandinavian immigration and intermarriage among the Sugpiaq people.
(Roy Corral)

Little Tim D. Melovedoff, Jr., plays among the tidepools. *(Roy Corral)*

designation was used on birth certificates well into the 20th century.

As the American period progressed, Native people realize they were not looked on as equals and many tried to find ways to secure their Native heritage. One way on Kodiak, where many had Russian surnames, was to emphasize their Russian backgrounds. My late uncle, Karl Armstrong, Jr., said people were taught that Creoles were "half as good as a Russian and twice as good as a Native." Therefore it was desirable to identify as a Russian if possible. My mother, Olga Vasilie Rossing, for example, was listed as a "Creole" on her birth certificate. As an adult she would identify herself first as a Russian and secondly as a Native. She was born in 1916 in the Sugpiaq village of Woody Island (*Tangirnaq*) to Vasili Rossing and Afanasiia Rysev. Rossing, of course, is not a Russian surname, but her father was born in 1885 as Vasili Shmakov and later adopted the name Rossing from his stepfather, Anton Rossing, after his natural father, Ivan Shmakov, died.

At one of the arch-aeological presentations of

The Native Village of Akhiok is located on the southern end of Kodiak Island and accessible only by air and water. The community's Russian Orthodox church, Protection of the Theotokos Chapel, dates to about 1900, when it was built on the site of an earlier church. *(Roy Corral)*

Stella Zeeder harvests sea urchins at low tide. *(Roy Corral)*

woven spruce baskets, and other tools. She said, almost to herself, "I guess we really are Natives after all. I was always told that we were Russians."

These identifications came back to haunt people after the Alaska Native Claims Settlement Act (ANCSA) was passed in 1971, and anyone with one quarter or more Native blood was eligible to enroll. Many of those emphasizing Russian heritage, whom had "passed" for non-Natives to gain social and economic acceptance within the dominant society, now enrolled as Natives, as they were legally entitled to do. This caused a backlash among other Natives that, to some degree, remains today. One way to insult someone is to say, "He (she) was never a Native until 1971."

The passage of ANCSA produced yet another identity, that of "shareholder." The regional corporation established under the act for the Kodiak area is called Koniag, Inc., and the term "Koniag shareholder" is one of the contemporary descriptive terms for Native people from this area. Even the name chosen for the corporation is reflective of a confused identity. The name "Koniag" does not ever seem to have been used as a self-designator. It is apparently derived from *Kanaagin*, the name applied to people of Kodiak Island by their traditional enemies, the Unangaˆx (Aleut) of the Aleutian Islands. The Sugpiaq, incidentally, had another name for the Unangaˆx—*Taya'ut*—a name of unknown origin that may simply mean "other" or "outsider." Some Sugpiaq elders recall that it was once considered a derogatory term.

So how did the Sugpiat come to call themselves Aleuts? The term apparently originated in Siberia as "Aliutor," a name applied to a coastal indigenous group on the Kamchatka Peninsula. Russian explorers thought the people they encountered in Alaska were the same, since their ways of life appeared similar, and applied this name first to the Unangaˆx and then to the Sugpiat. Like the descriptive terms "Indian" and "Eskimo" also applied by misunderstanding outsiders, Aleut stuck.

Further confusing the names and identity issue is

The village of Akhiok.
(Roy Corral)

the practice used from the Sugpiaq area of naming people as inhabitants of a certain place. This is done by adding the suffix "miut" meaning "people of" to a place name. Examples are *Qik'rtarmuit*, which refers to all people residing on Kodiak Island and means "people of the island," or *Sun'aqmiut*, meaning "people of Kodiak," or *Nuniaqmiut*, "people of Old Harbor." People can only use one of these terms if they physically reside at that location.

The revival of the pride in Sugpiaq heritage on Kodiak Island has made great strides over the past two to three decades. People are being assigned traditional names by Elders as a way of celebrating their Sugpiaq identity. The culture has become much more visible as all villages now have traditional dance groups and children are learning many traditional skills including carving masks, weaving baskets, and making Sugpiaq clothing. Summer culture camps involving Elders and youth are now a common occurrence.

The Alutiiq Museum in

Kodiak has established itself as model of cultural self-determination and sponsors many cultural activities including outreach programs to the villages. The museum is leading the effort to revive *Sugt'stun*, the Sugpiaq language. Sven Haakanson, Jr. (*Iqqaluk*), a Sugpiaq from the village of Old Harbor with a Ph.D. in anthropology from Harvard, has been the director since 2000. Among his many accomplishments is the coordination of a Spring 2008 exhibit of Sugpiaq masks, collected by Frenchman Alphonse Pinart in 1871, that have been in France since then and returning to Kodiak for the first time.

The issue of what the indigenous people of Kodiak Island should properly call themselves has greatly evolved in recent years. While it is still common to hear "Aleut" or "Alutiiq," an increasing number are opting for the original name of "Sugpiaq." This would

please the late Nina Olson, who grew up in the village of Afognak, who said, "I don't remember that we use the terms 'Aleut' or 'Alutiiq' to describe ourselves. We said 'Sugpiaq, a real person.' I think we should

go back to calling ourselves Sugpiaq. It has so much more meaning."

Whatever name is ultimately decided on, it will be decided by the people themselves and not by others.

Gordon Pullar with a mask in progress.
(Rick Knecht)

Gordon L. Pullar
(***Tan'icak***)*, a Kodiak Island Sugpiaq currently living in Anchorage, is an assistant professor and the director of the Department of Alaska Native and Rural Development at the University of Alaska Fairbanks. He has been involved in tribal self-determination and cultural revitalization efforts for the past three decades, including serving six years as president and CEO of the Kodiak Area Native Association. He is currently the president of the Woody Island Tribal Council in Kodiak and the chair of the Native American Advisory Group for the national Advisory Council on Historic Preservation. He co-edited (with Aron Crowell and Amy Steffian) the book,* Looking Both Ways: Heritage and Identity of the Alutiiq People.* He holds a Ph.D. in organizational anthropology and international studies.*

Yup'ik

Traditional
Homeland:
Yup'ik

Many children still grow up speaking Yup'ik at home.

Every March, hundreds of people arrive for Camai Dance Festival in Bethel, a Yup'ik regional hub near the mouth of the Kuskokwim River. They come from villages throughout the region, toting fancy parkas and headdresses trimmed in wolf and wolverine fur, and stands ruffled with tufts of caribou hair, seal-gut drums, and maybe a few newly carved wooden masks. Most come by airplane and snowmachine, but it least a few hook up their dog teams for brisk journeys across the delta's frozen rivers and sloughs. At night, the sound of howling sled dogs echo through the town, and ethereal chorus to the beating of dance drums and Yup'ik words raised in song.

Gathering such as this occurring towns and villages throughout Alaska's Yup'ik region, often in wintertime when people are generally less busy with fishing, hunting, and gathering activities and only have jobs and schools to plan around. Community potlatches and dance festivals bring people together, providing important cultural links spanning generations.

Wearing traditional kuspuks of cotton, Natalia Nayamin of Chevak (center), with her two daughters, Agnes Sweeden and Rebecca Nayamin, were selling handmade dolls, jewelry and kuspuks at a Native arts and crafts show during Anchorage's Fur Rendezvous. Natalia Nayamin's dolls depict various subsistence activities, such as berry picking, fishing, or gathering greens. The doll in the lower left is an old woman "pulling the last tooth," said Sweeden. *(Tricia Brown)*

At Kwigillingok, board-walks connect homes and schools and serve as sidewalks above the marshy tundra. The traditional Yup'ik village is part of the Lower Kuskokwim School District and has about 130 students and eight teachers. *(Andrea Pokrzywinski)*

Of all of Alaska's Native people, the Yup'ik are the most populous, with a booming birthrate, and have the largest number of individuals who still speak the language: nearly half of the Yup'ik population does. Most of them live in small villages along the Bering Sea coast and the lower Yukon and Kuskokwim Rivers. Outside the regional centers of Bethel (home to about 6,425 in 2010), Hooper Bay is the largest Yup'ik village—and one of the fastest-growing villages in Alaska—with 1,093 in 2010. Most Yup'ik villages are considerably smaller and tend to be made up of extended, interconnected families.

The Yup'ik traditional homelands extend south from Unalakleet River through the fan-shaped deltas of the Yukon and Kuskokwim Rivers and down along Bristol Bay, where Yup'ik culture eventually mingles with the Sugpiaq (Alutiiq) and Unanga^x (Aleut). In the Yup'ik stronghold of the Yukon Kuskokwim Delta, many children still grow up speaking Yup'ik at home. In perhaps seventeen of the sixty-eight Yup'ik villages, children learn Central Yup'ik as their first language. This is the most widely spoken Yup'ik language with about 14,000 speakers in the population of about 23,000. Local radio stations broadcast in the language, schoolchildren read Yup'ik texts, and in some places, elders can still converse in Yup'ik with their grandchildren. There are numerous dialects of Central Yup'ik, and although subtle variations exist between villages, sometimes giving slightly different meanings to the same word, most of the dialects are mutually intelligible.

Just as their ancestors were hunter-gatherers, so are modern Yup'ik people. Seasonal activities vary somewhat, depending on location, but may include hunting sea mammals such as seal, walrus, and whales; river fishing in summer for salmon and trout, and in winter for whitefish and tomcod; gathering wild vegetables, berries, and eggs; going into the uplands and mountains for ground squirrels, moose, and caribou; and harvesting ducks, geese, and other waterfowl that migrate by the millions each year into the Central Yup'ik region's rich wetlands, part of the Yukon Delta National Wildlife Refuge.

Still, Alaska's Yup'ik villages are hundreds of miles away from paved highways and urban centers, and while they are connected to the outside world by telephones, computers, and daily airplane flights, they remain largely self-contained bastions of Yup'ik culture. The region's many waterways are the Yup'ik road system, traveled by boats in summer and snowmachines or vehicles, mostly taxis, in winter.

Cash jobs are generally scarce, although some people in most

A Yup'ik craftsman works with a group of boys in a kayak-building class in this Hooper Bay photo dating from 1942. *(ASL-P306-0227, Alaska State Library, Evelyn Butler and George Dale Photographs)*

Basket weaver MaryAnn "Arnaucuaq" Sundown is among the elders who are teaching their craft to younger generations. *(Roy Corral)*

villages work for the state or village government, schools, or local stores.

Commercial salmon and herring fisheries give many villagers their only opportunities to earn money, so fishing, hunting, and gathering remain an integral part of life. While the subsistence harvest of fish, game, birds, greens, and berries is an economic and nutritional necessity, it is also much more: a lifestyle central to the Yup'ik culture. Connected to the acts of harvesting and gathering are traditional celebrations and stories, to which the people learn how to live and relate to the world around them.

In many respects, the Yup'ik live close to the ways of their ancestors while retaining their cultural identity in the context of the larger society. For instance, students from the Yupiit School District near Bethel have a presence on the Internet through collaboration with the University of Alaska's Oral History Program. Students at the district's three schools—Akiak, Akiachak, and Tuluksak—participated in Project Jukebox, recording photos, stories, and oral histories, demonstrating how traditional knowledge can be passed to the following generations using 21st-century technology.

Of all of Alaska's Native groups, the Yup'ik were among the last to experience prolonged contact with outsiders and generally were spared foreign intrusion until the early to mid-1800s. The Russians made limited explorations of Yup'ik country, with small expeditions along the Bering Sea coast and occasional forays upriver toward the Interior. The Russian Orthodox Church established a small mission and a few Russian trading posts were opened, including one in Norton Sound at St. Michael. This brought direct access to trade goods, and created a collector's market for Yup'ik-made items, such as coiled-grass baskets. But, for the most part, the Yup'iks were left alone until after the transfer of Alaska to the United States in 1867.

In the mid-1880s, salmon canneries opened on Bristol Bay, and Moravian missionaries arrived on the Kuskokwim River, where they established a church and school across from the Yup'ik village of *Mumtrekhlogamiut*; the missionaries called the new settlement "Bethel." The Catholics took the mouth of the Yukon River and later

Annie Blue, a Togiak Elder, is respected for her basket-weaving and skin-sewing, stitching fancy parkas, leggings, mukluks, and hats for dolls, children, as well as adults. Mrs. Blue, who was ninety-two in 2008, primarily speaks Yup'ik and looks to younger family members to translate English for her. The original site for Old Togiak was Togiagamute, across the bay from the present village location, which is now home to fewer than a thousand people. (Tricia Brown)

opened a mission at St. Mary's. As in many other parts of Alaska, the early missionaries spoke against the aboriginal belief systems and stifled many Yup'ik practices, which included making spirit masks to seek bountiful harvests, and holding potlatch feasts and dance celebrations to honor the spirits of people and animals.

Generally, however the inner delta had few resources to attract explorers. Even during the early 20th century, when gold discoveries brought droves of newcomers to parts of western Alaska, most of

Herring is woven into grass "garlands" to dry on outdoor racks. Here Susie Angiak collects the fish for storage. (Roy Corral)

Facing page: The village of Twin Hills, near the mouth of the Twin Hills River, was founded in 1965 when a few families left Togiak to avoid its repeated flooding problems. Other families moved here from Quinhagek. Flooding is a perennial issue for villagers along the Yukon and Kuskokwim Rivers, as well as their tributaries. (Ralph Andrew/DCRA)

the Yup'ik territory was basically ignored except for river corridors. It wasn't until the Alaska Native Claims Settlement Act (1971) and oil development on the North Slope (1970s) that the Yup'ik villages fully felt the grip of modern society. The land claims settlement, combined with the state's windfall of oil revenues, brought rapid change—modern housing, electricity, telephones, daily air service to regional centers, and in some cases, running water and sewage systems.

In recent years, several major religious denominations have apologized for denouncing Alaska's Native ways as pagan, and the Yup'ik have embraced their cultural dances and feasting with unbridled enthusiasm. In 1964, when Father René Astruc, S.J. arrived as administrator to St. Mary's Mission, he sent out word that he had no objection to potlatches. Within a year, the first was held. Now the potlatches and dance festivals draw villages together regularly, occurring almost as often as, and sometimes simultaneously with, community basketball tournaments.

"People realize you must have dancing," said Andrew Kelly of Emmonak. "Sometimes we have dancing every night. The dancing spirit is alive. It's very much alive today."

Torin Kuiggpak Jacobs of Bethel sorely missed Yup'ik dancing when he was away from home, attending Loyola University in Chicago. "I take so much pride in dancing the songs that my grandparents have danced and sang, and their grandparents and their

grandparents before them," Jacobs said. "Not only is it the pride, but the extreme spiritual feeling I receive. At dance festivals, when a member of the audience yelled '*pumyaa*' (bum-e-yaw, meaning "encore") I would gladly repeat the dance with all the energy I had left, to please the audience, myself, and my people."

Other elements of Yup'ik culture alive and visible today come from the traditional skills of carving, skin-sewing, and basket-making. Yup'ik people still make many cultural items for their own use, such as blackfish traps, spear points, fur boots, parkas, and dance fans. Likewise, they're made for sale to collectors of Native art. The Yup'ik have also encouraged continuation of their language by including bilingual and Yup'ik immersion in programs in their schools. The less visible aspects of Yup'ik culture, as for the other Native cultures and Alaska, are the beliefs shaping their view of the world. The missionaries did their work well in rural Alaska, converting people with a passion that has brought generations of devout followers. But at the same time, the Yup'ik, like other Natives, have recognized that their ancestor's cosmology was not exclusive of Christianity and that many of the basic values espoused by the Christian doctrines were also integral to Native spirituality. Reciprocity, sharing, and conscious awareness are such elements of the Yup'ik worldview.

In 2008, the Calista Elders Council and the Anchorage Museum

For Russian Orthodox believers, Christmas arrives on January 7 in Lower Kalskag and other towns throughout Alaska *(Roy Corral)*

James Gump of Hooper Bay uses marine mammal hide to make Yup'ik-style drums, which are struck from behind with a wooden wand. *(Roy Corral)*

hosted a major exhibition titled "Yuungnaqpiallerput (The Way We Genuinely Live): Masterworks of Yup'ik Science and Survival." Curated by anthropologist and author Ann Fienup-Riordan, displays included traditional tools and clothing, Yup'ik technology and other lifeways. Visitors gained insight into enduring Yup'ik truths—what traditional knowledge says about building and protecting relationships between individuals, communities, animals, and land.

"Things are not always what they seem . . . many possibilities exist, and we are not to be indifferent to other people's needs," explained Elsie Mather, Yup'ik linguist and author of *Cauyarniuq: A Time for Drumming*. "Everything on Earth deserves recognition, care, and respect."

Yup'ik Dance Masks: Stories of Culture

A group of school children gathered around a wooden nepcetaq mask, its smiling mouth lined with what looked like real teeth. The face had tear-shaped eye-holes with a third eye, pegged with teeth, on its forehead. The rounded yua, or spirit face, emerged from the feather-studded back-board, carved to represent the universe, water, air and land. Holes in the backboard showed passages through which the animals move in their journey toward the human hunter. The mask had been crafted under direction of an angalkuq, a powerful person, for which a special purpose—perhaps to predict the future or to call forth or show gratitude to the animals. When presented in dance, it would have appeared quite animated, symbolizing the union of the seen and unseen. Now stripped of its original use and purpose, and mounted behind protective glass, a century removed from its context, the mask still held its mysteries.

The unique mask was part of a greater collection of more than 200 Yup'ik dance masks in an exhibit called *Agayuliyararput* (Our Way of Making Prayer), which toured Alaska and the Lower 48 from 1996–98. The masks were collected from south-western Alaska around the turn of the century by missionaries and other visitors. They wound up in museums around the world, where little was known about them except where, when and by whom they were collected. Now, however, a great deal more information is known, thanks to the Alaska Yup'ik community and exhibit curator Ann Fienup-Riordan, an anthropologist well-respected for her work and writings about Yup'ik culture.

Agayuliyararput was more than simply an exhibit of objects; it represented a collection of stories about the masks and Yup'ik culture as told by Yup'ik people. A committee of Yup'ik men and women worked closely with Fienup-Riordan and museum specialists.

In 1996, some of the masks returned for a time to their place of origin when the exhibit debuted in the southwestern Alaska village of Toksook Bay. More than 500 Yup'ik people flew into Toksook Bay the day the exhibit opened, to see the masks, to dance and feast.

The exhibit then moved to the Yupiit Picirarait Cultural Center in Bethel for a two-month stay; then to the Anchorage Museum of History and Art. From there, *Agayuliyararput* moved onward to Juneau and Fairbanks, into the National Museum of the American Indian in New York, and finally, to the National Museum of Natural History at Smithsonian Institution.

Crucial to presenting the masks was collecting stories about them from Yup'ik Elders. These elders were some of the last survivors of a time when Yup'ik life still included masked dances in the *qasgiq*, or men's house, where the males of the winter village lived separately from the females. Marie Meade, a Yup'ik language specialist raised in Nunapitchuk, brought pictures of the masks into the homes of Yup'ik Elders. She recorded, then translated, their tales. Some of the Elders remembered who made particular masks; others remembered seeing the masks used; still others recalled various related happenings. Meade's thirty hours of taped interviews became the basis for many of the exhibit interpretive materials. Condensed versions of the Elders stories are presented in the Yup'ik and English in *Kegginaqut, Kangiit-Ilu (Yup'ik Masks and the Stories They Tell)* by Meade and Fienup-Riordan. Another essential companion book is Fienup-Riordan's comprehensive catalog, *The Living Tradition of Yup'ik Masks*.

The exhibit amplified what started in 1989 when a group of old Yup'ik masks were borrowed from the Sheldon Jackson Museum in Sitka and exhibited during a regional dance festival held in Mountain Village. Elders and community leaders had wanted to revive Yup'ik culture among young people with the display of artifacts during the festival, to show how their ancestors lived. Andy Paukan, from St. Mary's, helped bring the masks back that time and worked closely with Fienup-Riordan to mount *Agayuliyararput*.

In the late 1990s, Paukan spoke about the exhibit's significance: "This project is important to me and, I believe, for all Yup'ik people, not just because it brings the past back to us but because it may preserve our future. . . . I consider it fortunate that so many well-regarded museums have fine coll-ections of Yup'ik materials collected at an important time in our history. Certainly those who collected these items may have thought they were collecting the artifacts of a vanishing culture. However, among those of us whose forefathers were the craftsmen, these items demonstrate that we may be different, but we have not vanished."

Siberian Yupik

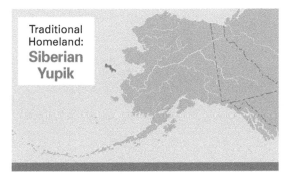

Traditional
Homeland:
**Siberian
Yupik**

From St. Lawrence Island, Siberia is a mere thirty-eight miles away.

In Alaska, Siberian Yupik is spoken exclusively on St. Lawrence Island, where almost all Native residents still speak it, and it is the first language their children learn. Siberian Yupik is a unique language, mostly unintelligible to speakers of Central Yup'ik, and is also spoken by a small group of Natives at the southern tip of the Chukotsk Peninsula in Russia.

St. Lawrence Island is located about 200 miles southwest from Nome on the Alaska mainland. From the island, Siberia is a mere thirty-eight miles away. Its two large communities are Savoonga, with a population of 704 in 2011, and Gambell, home to 711 people.

Facing page: Delma Apassingok cuts a snack of whale meat for daughter, Jani, as husband, Edmond, talks on the phone. *(Roy Corral)*

William Soonagrook, Jr., of Gambell represents the art of other Siberian Yupik carvers as well as his own work. A large percentage of the hunters on St. Lawrence are also carvers. *(Tricia Brown)*

Walrus meat is cut and hung to dry on outdoors racks in Gambell. *(Nicole Grewe/DCRA)*

Alaska's Siberian Yupik rarely engage in inland activities and depend mostly on marine mammals for food and cultural traditions. Like Alaska's other Native peoples they, too, take advantage of the latest technology and use metal boats with outboard motors, snowmachines, and four-wheel all-terrain vehicles when suitable.

They hunt bowhead whales from open skin boats powered with sales, dividing up the meat and fat following customs that prescribe certain parts to the hunters, their families, and other villagers. Walrus is plentiful, and the people use every part of the animal, including the tusks, which artisans sculpt and carve for sale to collectors.

Above: Drifting snow mounds between rows of houses in the village of Gambell. (Nicole Grewe/DCRA)

Left: St. Lawrence Island whale hunters divide the meat and baleen to share among the villagers. (Chlaus Lotscher/ AlaskaStock)

Considering the island's small population, it's amazing that more than 100 hunters also engage in carving, using the whalebone, baleen, and ivory to craft small figures, both stylized and realistic, of the birds and animals they know so well. Due to their remote location, the hunter-carvers have formed a cooperative to promote their work and increase their presence at Alaska Native art shows and other venues.

Iñupiat

Traditional
Homeland:
Iñupiat

The Iñupiat are the northernmost Alaska Natives. They include bowhead whale hunters living along the Chukchi and Beaufort Sea coasts of the Arctic Ocean, who launch skin-covered boats into ice-choked waters to chase, harpoon and drag ashore sixty-ton behemoths. They include polar bear, seal, and walrus hunters of Kotzebue Sound and the Seward Peninsula. They include salmon fishermen, reindeer herders, and caribou hunters along the coast, inland rivers, or in the arctic tundra of the Central Brooks Range. They include women skilled in sewing skins into boat covers, who can fashion fur garments to protect against instant frostbite in howling winter winds, who spend their days in their kitchens cooking up feasts of traditional, ceremonial and Western foods to feed entire villages.

In the 2010 census, 33,360 people nationwide reported they were Iñupiat or partly Iñupiat. A majority live in their traditional homelands—the northwest corner of Alaska and along the North Slope. Iñupiat villages and larger towns are located along the coastal areas and inland rivers, land on which their ancestors have lived for centuries.

A majority of the Iñupiat people live in their traditional homelands.

Young girls play with a Game Boy. *(Chris Arend/ AlaskaStock)*

Anaktuvuk Pass is home to inland Iñupiat people, who differ in their subsistence hunting—catching caribou, moose, and bear rather than sea mammals. Instead the inland and coastal people trade with each other. *(Guido Keel/DCRA)*

Barrow, the northernmost city in Alaska, is one of those old Iñupiat trading sites, known among the people by its Eskimo name, *Ukpeagvik*. Its population in the 2010 census number 4,212, with more than 60 percent claiming Native heritage. Barrow is home to Arctic Slope Regional Corp., perhaps the wealthiest Native corporation in the state, and headquarters for the North Slope Borough. It's a place where whaling captains are as comfortable in the corporation's mirrored-glass office tower as in their skin *umiats* on the ocean. Tucked down around the coast off Bering Strait sits Kotzebue, a largely Iñupiat town of 3,201 with nearly 74 percent of its population all or part Native. Kotzebue serves as the regional and commercial center for northwest Alaska.

The Iñupiat region extends south to encompass the Seward Peninsula to Unalakeet River. It serves as the gold-mine town of Nome, populated in 2010 by 3,598 people, more than half of whom were Iñupiat.

Westernization has come to Iñupiat villages in various forms and degrees during the last two decades, blending with the remnants of earlier times. Many efforts are being made in Iñupiat towns and villages to strengthen cultural connections, such as Iñupiat language and culture programs in the schools. In Barrow, for instance, signs throughout the city are written in Iñupiaq as well as English, and the local radio station broadcasts some of the programs in Iñupiaq.

"Our Elders have always told us that if we lose our language, we'll lose our culture," said Fanny Akpik, an assistant professor at Ilisagvik College in Barrow. Her voice is familiar to listeners at KBRW radio. Sprinkled into the public radio programming for local station KBRW is the Iñupiaq "Word of the Day," and an Iñupiaq story hour is broadcast each weeknight. Disc jockey James Patkotak translates information into the Iñupiaq language for his listeners, too. Most fluent speakers of Iñupiaq are Elders or middle-aged adults.

In recent years, Akpik and other North Slope Borough School District Inupiaq language teachers traveled to Montana to learn new ways of teaching language skills. Their instructor, Arapaho professor Dr. Stephen Neyooxet Greymorning, steered them away from translating names of objects, concepts, and books taken from the Western culture. Instead, the teachers revolutionized their approach by going back to basics in their own culture. Greymorning led them to create foundational word lists—human terms, animals, transportation, and objects—to match photos based on life on the North Slope. From there, the group laid out their teaching plan based

"... if we lose our language, we'll lose our culture."

Four-wheelers at post office, Point Hope.
(Harry Walker/AlaskaStock)

Man in fur ruff parka on Arctic Ocean near Point Barrow. *(Jeff Schultz/ AlaskaStock)*

on logical developmental progression for their students. Recounting Greymorning's incredible success with the method elsewhere, the NSBSD also reported on its Web site: "At the conclusion of the workshop, in time-honored Iñupiaq fashion the group 'adopted' Neyooxet by bestowing him with the Inupiaq name of Nuyaagiq as chosen by Ilisagvik College assistant professor of Iñupiaq Studies, Fannie Akpik. He was presented with gifts of appreciation and gratitude consisting of a baleen whale made by Lucy Richards, a selection of Iñupiaq children's stories and the men and women's whaling standards. In a moving spiritual moment, the group sang the Iñupiaq version of 'How Great Thou Art' as the final tribute to Nuyaagiq who, truly, has given the Iñupiaq teachers a way to give the gift of language."

The Iñupiat people can trace their ancestry to the beginning of time in their stories; archaeologists have chased them back thousands of years in Alaska, to camping and trading sites used by some of the first Iñupiat ancestors to enter from Asia. One of the oldest sites is Onion Portage on the Kobuk River. Archaeological finds in northern Alaska show progression of cultural adaptations and change that includes hunting large mammals, netting fish, and spearing caribou. About 2,500 years ago, Iñupiat ancestors started hunting seals and other sea mammals. Whaling technologies appeared about 1,500 years ago. One of the oldest whaling settlements was at Point Hope. Coastal camps grew into large settlements, as people cooperated to harvest the large sea mammals. Eventually, someone started fishing with hooks and lines, and people moved inland to live by lakes

The people can trace their ancestry to the beginning of time.

Iñupiat drummers from Wainwright. *(Chris Arend/ AlaskaStock)*

Basket-maker Minnie
Gray of Ambler shapes
birch bark into beautiful,
functional pieces of art.
(Roy Corral)

and rivers. The introduction of the sinew bow from Asia gave new efficiency to caribou hunting. About 500 years ago people started harnessing dogs to work pulling sleds.

In 1998, the Kotzebue Elders founded a cultural camp, Camp Pipe Spit, as a place to mentor youngsters. In a setting eleven miles north of the city, along the coast, students were introduced to traditional hunting and fishing, plant identification and medicinal value, language, cultural history and stories, and more. Among the teaching Elders was Elmer Goodwin. As a youngster, Goodwin learned much from his grandparents, who taught him by example such things as setting snares for rabbits and using dogsleds.

"When outboards (motors) came, they taught me how to do that. Then snowmachines came. There's been a lot of changes since I've been alive—modern houses, telephones, cars in the village."

Goodwin lived in Los Angeles for eleven years after graduating from high school. He wanted to experience "life with white man in his own environment." He attended welding school, worked as a construction foreman and clerked in a furniture store. But he missed "my people, my Native food . . . the seals, fish, dried fish, and meat. And I missed my language. There was nobody to talk to down there." Each summer, he returned to his village to visit. Finally, he returned for good and began teaching Iñupiaq language, values, and crafts, as well as traditional hunting and fishing.

Tuapaktusuk Culture Camp near Barrow, sponsored by Ilisagvik College, was launched in the summer of 2006 as another important place for Elders to pass along skills and words of knowledge. And although Iñupiat youth are the target audience, they are not the only ones to benefit from culture camps. Through the Rose Urban Rural Exchange, teachers from Anchorage, Fairbanks, and schools in the Matanuska-Susitna Valley spend a portion of their summer in a rural town or village to gain understanding of Native culture by experiencing it for themselves.

Whaling figures prominently in the history of the Iñupiat region. In the late 1840s, American whalers sailed to the Bering Strait region

in the first big wave of outsiders. They brought trade goods and employed some Iñupiat whalers seasonally. They also brought disease and alcohol. Although few whalers settled in the region, their impact was long-lived.

Today's subsistence whaling remains a strong and visible aspect of Iñupiat culture. Hunting large creatures from a small craft in the polar seas is dangerous and requires an immeasurable seafaring skills and core operation between boats. The entire community spends months preparing gear, clothing, and food for the cruise. Once landed, the whale is divided among crewmembers, and shares are given to Elders, families without hunters and sometimes sent to relatives in cities. Throughout the year, whale is shared at festivals, holidays, and other special occasions.

Subsistence bowhead whaling has undergone numerous modifications in recent decades. The International Whaling

An aerial view of Barrow, the most northern city in the United States, during spring breakup. *(Steven Kaslowski/ AlaskaStock)*

A Barrow man uses a handmade fleshing tool to begin the butchering process. *(Roy Corral)*

Commission determines a quota for hunting, based on the strength of the whale population. At their 2007 meeting, held in Anchorage, the Commission determined that from 2008 to 2012, the Native people of Alaska and Chukotka (Russia) could land up to 280 bowhead whales, with no more than sixty-seven whales struck in any one year. The Alaska Eskimo Whaling Commission then divided the Alaska quota among the whaling villages, allotting each a certain number of "strikes," or attempts. The villages include Barrow, Nuiqsut, Kaktovik, Point Hope, Wainwright, Kivalina, Wales, Savoonga, Gambell, and Little Diomede.

Even though whaling is closely associated with Iñupiat culture, the majority of Iñupiat villages are not directly involved with hunting bowheads. However hunting for beluga whales, walrus, and bearded and ringed seals remains important to most of the villages. Spring harvests in the Kotzebue Basin focus on bearded and ringed seals off Cape Krusenstern and Cape Espenberg. Beluga hunters pitch tents along the beach at Elephant Point on Eschscholtz Bay, where belugas feed on spawning smelt.

What Iñupiat people do largely depends on the season and available resources. In addition to sea mammals, villagers may harvest caribou, polar, and grizzly bears, musk oxen, whitefish, waterfowl, salmon, smelt, arctic char, waterfowl, berries, and wild vegetables. Subsistence activities are culturally important and often provide most of the family's nutritional needs. Subsistence can be a full-time job, but many people also need cash wage employment to pay expenses. They find work, often seasonal, at local schools, in government and small businesses, and commercial fishing and construction, and in the North Slope oil fields or the Red Dog Mine, a zinc mining operation near Kotzebue.

Some Iñupiat are involved in herding reindeer, domestic cousins to caribou. In the 1890s, Sheldon Jackson, then Superintendent of Education for Alaska, introduced reindeer as a food source and wage-earning occupation for Seward Peninsula Natives. They learned animal husbandry from Scandinavians who were

Maligian Hopson helps divide shares of whale meat. *(Roy Corral)*

An Iñupiaq whaling captain and artist, Simeon Patkotak, Sr., was selling bowhead whale baleen for his grandson at a Native arts and crafts show in Anchorage. While many shoppers inquired about buying the baleen basket that his grandson made, Patkotak said it was for display only—an example of what skilled hands can make with baleen. Baleen is found in the whale's mouth and used to filter seawater for krill and other marine organisms that feed the animals. *(Tricia Brown)*

brought to Alaska specifically to teach the Iñupiat. A law that passed in 1937 restricted reindeer ownership to Natives, and while there were still about a dozen permit holders in the mid-1990s, herding is on the decline today as the stocks have integrated with the growing influx of caribou. Some tens of thousands of caribou extended their westward migration range and virtually absorbed the roughly 25,000 reindeer on the Seward Peninsula. However, herders who lost animals remain hopeful that they can round up their stocks again and continue this century-old tradition. Reindeer handling blends with subsistence activities. In spring, the herders monitor calving. In June, using helicopters to round up the animals, they harvest antlers for mostly Asian markets. In early winter, the herders on snowmachines catch and butcher the steers. Much of the meat is processed commercially and sold as sausage.

In Anaktuvuk Pass in the central Brooks Range, caribou is the primary food. Many items are made from the skins, including masks. In earlier times people walked from Anaktuvuk Pass to the coasts to trade caribou skins and fur pelts for seal oil. Today traveling by airplane, people take great pleasure in sharing their subsistence foods and handiwork with friends and relatives in other villages.

And at Barrow, a big trade fair with ancient traditions has once again become a much-anticipated annual event. The festival, *Kivgiq*, is held in midwinter, drawing hundreds of people from across the North Slope to dance, eat, trade items, sell crafts, exchange gifts, tell stories and play games. In recent years, dancers from as far away as Russia, Canada, and Hawaii have joined the celebration.

After hearing elders reminisce about the old "messenger feast," last held in 1914, Borough Mayor George Ahmaogak sparked its return in 1988.

"Iñupiat dance, which had long been a dying art, was the centerpiece of Kivgiq," wrote *Anchorage Daily News* columnist Elise Patkotak, who lived in Barrow for thirty years. "Interest in traditional dance was revived because, without a dance group, you didn't have anyone to represent your village at the festival. And there was not one

Families on the Seward Peninsula have been herding reindeer since as early as 1894.
(Roy Corral)

village on the North Slope that wanted to be left out.

"There are now as many as two to three dance groups in villages where once there had been barely one. Traditional dances such as the Kaluqaq, which had not been seen for decades, are again being performed. With the renewed interest in the dance, came renewed interest in the cultural history it carried. . . . [Amhaogak] gave young people a chance to learn pride in their traditions—traditions that had seemingly been on the brink of extinction."

A Time for Whaling

By Sheila Frankson

I am an Iñupiat Eskimo from Point Hope, although I now live in Barrow. My home village of about 678 people is located on the northwest coast of Alaska is one of the state's oldest villages.

Springtime is our whaling season. When I was a teenager, I had my first experience out on the ice during whaling season with Calvin and Irma Oktollik. Even though I had grown up in Point Hope and joined every year in the work in celebration of whaling season, I'd never actually gone out to stay at a whaling camp. I was really excited!

During winter, snow falls and the wind blows. It gets really cold—temperatures reach -60°F, dropping to -80°F and -90°F with wind chill—and the ocean freezes. The Arctic Ocean has a permanent frozen mass called pack ice that can freeze to new ice during the winter sunlight is maybe light blue and some may be plain white. When you go out on the frozen ocean, you see a lot of big and small pieces of ice on top of each other.

To get ready for whaling, the men break trail through these jumbles of ice. They use certain tools such as ice picks, axes, and shovels. When they return to set their tent, they'll know which way to go. They make a trail all the way to the open lead—a place where the ice has broken apart into an open channel. The whales, who need air to breathe, travel these leads through the ice to their calving grounds. An open lead is usually several miles out from shore, although some years the lead can be seen from town.

While men break trail, the ladies used to sew sealskins together to make covers for the *umiaks*, the skin boats used for whaling. They sewed the skins together in a particular way with ivory needles and thick thread, so the skins wouldn't rip apart while the men are in the boat pursuing a whale.

We go to out tents at whaling camp on snowmachines pulling wooden sleds. Back in the old days (before the late 1960s), we didn't have cars or snowmachines. All we had were dogs and sleds for transportation. The village men still make the sleds to haul gear and *umiaks* out to the ice, and bring back *maktak* (muktuk) and whale meat. *Maktak* is the blubber and skin of the whale that my people consider a delicacy to eat.

When I went out on the ice, I had certain chores to do. They included washing dishes after every meal and keeping the area around and inside the inside of the tent clean. Some days, if the *boyars* (young boys who help around the tent) were not around, I also helped cut up driftwood and seal blubber to burn in the stove, and get snow to melt for drinking and washing if we were running out. The *boyar* also stayed up during the night and tended the stove while the hunters slept. When the whalers woke up, they went back out to the wind-breakers and looked for whales. The wind-breakers were pieces of ice that were set up at the edge of the lead. When you looked into the open water from beyond a breaker, you could see if the whales are passing by.

If the water closed up with ice and the lead disappeared, the crew-members returned to the village to wait for lead to open again.

Block and tackle, manpower, and a skiff's horsepower help to land a bowhead whale.
(Roy Corral)

Nalukataq is an Iñupiaq word for "blanket toss," one of the time-honored activities in the spring, a celebration recognizing a successful whale hunt. After shares of meat and blubber are divided among the people, the community comes together to celebrate. The "blanket" used in the blanket toss is made of sea mammal skins. Around its edge, thick rope is loosely laced, creating handles for people to hold. They stand shoulder to shoulder and flick one person high into the air. *(ASL-P320-36 , Alaska State Library, Reverend Samuel Spriggs. Photographs)*

When we went out on the ice, we weren't to use anything red because the color would scare the whales. We also had to wear warm clothing. When you're out there, it gets cold, even though some days are a little warm. You need such things as ski pants, boots, gloves or mittens, a couple pairs of socks, Eskimo jacket (parka with the ruff), and a hat.

After one of the crews caught a whale, everybody started yelling with excitement! Usually it takes at least a day to cut up a whale. The whale was harvested on the ice where it was landed. Back in town, the families of the crew and the captain gave out candy to celebrate. Everybody was welcome to take some. It's a tradition that's been going on for many years.

Whaling season ends for one of two reasons. Either we have reached the quota our village is given by the Alaska Eskimo Whaling Commission, or the ice is getting too rotten to stay out safely.

After whaling season was over, we waited for June to have a feast called

Nalukataq. We went out on the tundra outside of town by the whalebones that have been set up for a long time. This was the traditional place for our *Nalukataq*. We served food and gave a share of whales to everyone who came. It was a time for gathering and talking. People from different villages usually came to Point Hope every year for *Nalukataq* to celebrate with their friends and relatives.

On the first day, a village Elder said the little prayer before anyone ate. Then everybody ate, visited a while and went home. The next day, they returned and ate again. Afterward, they Eskimo danced and did the blanket toss.

The blanket was sealskins sewn together with rope handles around the edge. One person got on top of the skin blanket while other people grabbed the handles and bounced it to throw that person up in the air. While up in the air, that person kicked his or her legs as if running. Some people threw candy into the air while they were being tossed and everybody tried to get all the candy they could. I liked watching it.

As a teenager, I was slowly learning what it was like in the old days. But as I got older I realized that not being able to speak my Native language, *Iñupiaq*, was the problem. I wanted to learn Iñupiaq, but I found it hard to understand. I wanted to be able to communicate in Iñupiaq with our Elders in Point Hope, to have them tell me what it was like living in the old days. When our Elders talk in *Iñupiaq*, I listened to small words that I knew and tried to understand what they were saying. I'm hoping one day I will be able to talk to our Elders using my traditional language.

Our language and our traditions mean a lot to our Elders, and I know that they want to see that we learn it. On the other hand, trying to get everything ready for whaling and Nalukataq isn't that easy.

Although it's hard work, we Iñupiat never give up. We do our best, and if it means we have to keep on trying, then that's what we do. We'll do it over and over until we feel we've gotten it right.

After graduation from Tikigaq High School in Point Hope, **Sheila Frankson** *went on to take classes at Sheldon Jackson College and later moved to Barrow. Today she is a stay-at-home mother with three young boys to keep her busy. She looks forward to her sons learning more about their culture and language from the Elders as well as in the classroom. "My six-year-old started counting his numbers in Iñupiaq when he was three," she says with a smile in her voice.*

Athabascan

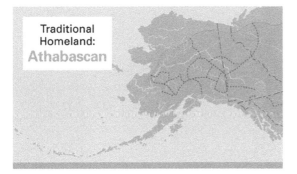

Traditional Homeland: Athabascan

Alaska's Athabascan people occupy the largest geographic area with the most diverse environment of any of Alaska's Native groups. Alaska's broad Interior is usually identified as the Athabascan heartland, but their homelands stretch from the Brooks Range south past the Alaska Range to Lake Iliamna, Cook Inlet, and the Kenai Peninsula.

The territory's mountains, rolling uplands, boreal spruce forests, valleys, lakes, wetlands, and coastal habitats all play a part in Athabascan culture and lore. But perhaps most pivotal to the Athabascan lifestyle have been the region's many waterways, including the mighty Yukon, Kuskokwim, Koyukuk, Tanana, Susitna, and Copper river systems. For centuries, Athabascans have traveled, traded, fished, hunted, trapped, and lived along these rivers and their tributaries. The rivers also brought explorers, traders, missionaries, and miners opening Athabascan country to an era of change still unfolding.

Athabascans represent one of the most widespread linguistic groups among Natives in North America. They extend from Alaska's

Tribal councils are an important form of village governance . . .

Facing page: Curious children from Arctic Village peer out at a new face in their village. *(Roy Corral)*

105

Subsistence hunting and fishing remain central to Athabascan culture.

Salmon runs in the Interior's great rivers are a mainstay for subsistence fishermen. Many villagers spent part of every summer at fish camp, where families live and work together to catch, cut, dry, and smoke salmon along the river's edge. *(Matt Hage/ AlaskaStock.com)*

Arctic through Canada to the Mexican border, and include the Navajo and Apache of the American southwest.

In the 2010 federal census, 15,623 people claimed they were Athabascan; another 6,861 had some Athabascan heritage. Many were living in remote villages accessible only by airplanes and boats, or snowmachines and dogsleds in winter. Village-operated diesel-powered generators provide electricity, but few homes have running water or flush toilets. Most villages have satellite communications, including television. Tribal councils are an important form of village governance, and Athabascan villages have been leaders in Native Alaska in asserting tribal powers under federal law.

People in Athabascan villages do a variety of things to make a living and obtain cash to buy ammunition and gasoline for boats and four-wheelers for subsistence activities. Some people hold government jobs such as teacher's aides and public health aides. Some summers, young adults can earn a decent income is fighting forest fires on public lands. Many people fish commercially for salmon and work construction. A growing list of communities—including Stevens Village, Huslia, and Eklutna—market themselves as tourist destinations for visitors interested in Native lifestyles.

Subsistence hunting and fishing remains central to Athabascan culture. People depend on salmon, whitefish, grayling, tomcod, moose, caribou, bear, beaver, hare, birds, berries, and edible plants. Upland villages not located on major salmon rivers rely substantially on migrating caribou and resident populations of moose.

"I live in Fairbanks and I still live off the land," said Amy Van Hatten, who grew up in Galena. As a city dweller, she would send fishnets and

In summer, four-wheelers allow access to hunting and fishing sites; in winter, the people rely on snow-machines (or sno-gos, as they're sometimes still called) to get around the backcountry. *(Wet Waders/ AlaskaStock.com)*

Ninilchik lies along Cook Inlet on the Kenai Peninsula, at a place the Dena'ina people had called *Niqnilchint,* for "lodge by the river." *(Nicole Grewe/DCRA)*

canning jars to relatives in the villages; they would send her salmon. Her backyard had a smokehouse, like those she'd have at fish camp, and she regularly dined on moose. She recalled one business trip to Washington, D.C., when her craving for moose meat was insatiable. "My physical nature depends on it," she said.

"We are a very rich culture, with a lot to be proud of. I go back (to the village) as often as I can. My roots are strong."

Athabascan people often identify themselves according to their home village. In a broader sense, the villages fall into linguistic territories corresponding to the eleven Athabascan languages traditionally spoken in Alaska—*Ahtna, Deg Hit'an, Holikachuk, Koyukon, Upper Kuskokwim, Dena'ina (Tanaina), Tanacross, Tanana, Upper Tanana, Hän,* and *Gwich'in.* These languages are, for the most part, not mutually intelligible, and most have more than one dialect. The greatest numbers of Native speakers are found among the Gwich'in and Koyukon—the largest of all of Alaska's Athabascan groups. The number of fluent speakers grows smaller each year; most are Elders. In only the most traditional villages do children speak the language, although fewer are learning in recent years.

Daisy Demientieff of Grayling is renowned for her beadwork and baskets. She is the daughter of another skilled craftswoman, Belle Deacon, born in Anvik in 1904, who likewise learned from her mother and grandmother. *(Tricia Brown)*

Their Athabascan ancestors, some linguists call Na-Dene, were among the latter waves of people to come into Alaska from Asia. Small groups, perhaps following herds of bison, elk, caribou, and mammoths, crossed the Bering Sea land bridge exposed by lower Ice-Age ocean levels. These ancient people also fished and hunted small mammals and birds, according to archaeological findings of late Ice-Age camps, such as the Broken Mammoth site on Tanana River. Some linguists suggest that east-central Alaska and Canada's Yukon Territory served as the Na-Dene homeland. As groups of Na-Dene went their separate ways over time, different languages and cultures evolved including Athabascan, Eyak, and Tlingit.

Until about the last 100 years the Athabascan people in Alaska lived a seminomadic existence, moving seasonally from camp to camp. They lived in small groups often composed of extended family and led by the most skillful and accomplished hunter, usually a man with considerable spiritual powers. Generally the groups remained independent of each other as they moved about, building temporary shelters with branches and moose hides. Sometimes they built more permanent structures from bark, moss, or sod. In some places the Athabascans adopted technology from their neighbors; for instance the Deg Hit'an in southwestern Alaska borrowed ideas from the Yup'ik, such as masked dancing and communal structures with benches and fire pits for winter camps. The Dena'ina—the only Athabascans in Alaska to live on saltwater and hunt sea mammals such as sea lions and the beluga whales—used kayaklike boats common to the Sugpiaq

Facing page: Temperatures in Athabascan country have reached the highest highs and the lowest lows on record in Alaska. Fort Yukon hit 100°F in 1915, and Prospect Creek, a camp along the trans-Alaska pipeline, experienced -80°F in 1971 (without wind-chill applied). *(AlaskaStock.com)*

Three Athabascan men posed for Charles O. Farciot, who accompanied the Schieffelin brothers in their prospecting trip of 1882-1883. Farciot labeled the image, "Sinate, Chief of Fort Yukon Indians, Mrs. Mayo's father." White trader Alfred Mayo, who arrived in the Yukon River Basin in 1873, married Sinate's daughter Margaret the following year. The couple opened a trading post at Rampart in 1897. *(ASL-P277-017-016, Alaska State Library, Wickersham Historic Site)*

(Alutiiq), who frequented Cook Inlet to hunt and raid Dena'ina villages.

Despite their relative autonomy, various Athabascan groups came together each year for trade and festivities; sometimes they traded with the Eskimos. For instance the Ahtna came down the Matanuska River Valley to trade with the Dena'ina on Cook Inlet; the Gwich'in who settled Arctic Village used to track 300 miles through the Brooks Range to the Arctic coast, to obtain seal oil from the Iñupiat, trading sinew, wolverine skins, and spruce pitch. The community of Tanana still holds the festival each June to commemorate ancient Athabascan trade gatherings at nearby *Nuchalawoya*, a site at the confluence of the Tanana and Yukon rivers.

In the late 1700s, Europeans started appearing in Athabascan territory. The Russians ventured into Dena'ina territory on Cook Inlet and Ahtna country on the lower Copper River in the 1780s, then filtered west to the Kuskokwim River and by the 1840s penetrated the lower Yukon River. Meanwhile, Hudson's Bay Co. fur traders floated down the Yukon River out of Canada, establishing Fort Yukon in 1847. The traders introduced material goods, guns, and Western foods such as sugar, tea, and alcohol. Hudson's Bay Co. traders also brought

Located on the south shore of the Kvichak River, Igiugig it is today considered a Sugpiaq (Alutiiq) village, although this was historically a region occupied by Kiatagmuit Eskimos. The present village grew when people from the village of Branch relocated at the turn of the last century. *(Tricia Brown)*

fiddles, and the Gwich'in and Koyukon people adopted their French–Canadian and Scottish tunes. A distinct style of Athabascan fiddle-playing evolved, additionally influenced by string music brought later by other outsiders. Today, the musical legacy is enjoyed at village dances and each November in Fairbanks, during the Athabascan Old-Time Fiddling Festival.

The Athabascans also encountered military expeditions, missionaries, and gold prospectors who fanned out along the rivers of the Interior. In more than one instance, Athabascans saved the newcomers from starvation or freezing by sharing their food, fires, and knowledge of the land. Lt. Henry Allen, who mapped the Copper, Tanana, and Koyukuk rivers, wrote admiringly in 1885 of a boat—"one of the heartiest small crafts I've ever seen"—made for his crew by an Ahtna on the Copper River. The man bound willow shoots with rawhide strings and covered the frame in moose hides sewed with sinew.

On the Yukon River, the Roman Catholics established a mission at Holy Cross and Nulato, and the Episcopalians at Anvik. These and other missionaries encouraged the Athabascans to establish year-round villages, so their children could be formally educated in mission schools.

That's how the village of Old Minto originated on the east bank of the Tanana River, said Neil Charlie. His grandfather, Chief Charlie, settled his band there in 1913, at the behest of preachers. Even so, the people continued going to fishing and hunting camps. Neil Charlie said his parents usually came back to the village during the school year; he attended through fifth grade. In 1970, after five consecutive years of flooding, the villagers relocated twenty miles north to higher ground on the Tolovana River.

Neil Charlie left the village as a young man to see how other people lived. He moved to Tanacross, where he worked several years as postmaster, than to Fairbanks where he worked on a military base and later for Tanana Chiefs Conference, the nonprofit health and social services agency for the Interior. In the late 1980s, Charlie set up the nonprofit Cultural Heritage Education Institute. His goal: to bring people together and offer opportunities for Athabascan youth to learn more about their culture.

"By understanding how other people have lived, they can find their own way better," he said.

Old Minto is the site of a cultural camp where Elders share traditional knowledge with Natives and non-Natives. Some of the camps are geared toward young people; others are for teachers to acquaint them with the cultural background of Native students in villages or urban areas. One of the institute's more recent projects was to document Athabascan place-names and stories for locations in the Minto Flats.

A number of similar cultural revitalization efforts are going on throughout Athabascan country.

"Typical of a lot of indigenous cultures in mainstream America, there's a growing concern about our culture adapting to change," said Will Mayo, a former president of Tanana Chiefs. "There are

Although the "lakes region" of Southwestern Alaska is home to Athabascan, Sugpiaq, and Yup'ik people, the majority of modern Nondalton's population is Athabascan.
(Tricia Brown)

tremendous pressures from outside forces on the Athabascan culture. The people recognize that cultures are dynamic and changing; but the question is: Are they changing in ways we can control and manage?"

"Some of the deep aspects of our culture are disappearing. . . . Language is the real obvious one. The only people who speak fluently are the Elders, and even they say few know the 'high language.' You can imagine the loss that represents to the depth and understanding of our culture. But also the ancient skills—how people live, the clothing and crafts, the making and use of tools and hunting weapons. And storytelling, the method of transmitting cultural standards and values. People are concerned that television is becoming the storyteller, passing on values, principles, and morals that aren't Athabascan.

"Yet I go to villages and see children with strong cultural values . . . young people who know old songs and dances and cultural practices. Our culture is strongest in the villages where children are with their parents, where their parents are teaching them daily about their culture . . . Even in my home in the city, we practice the culture in ways we don't even notice, because it's bred into us . . . in the way that we talk about animals and the simple process of going out to hunt, about the way you should conduct yourself, what's right and wrong, what to stay away from, what to pursue."

Years ago, as a featured speaker during Alaska Federation of Natives annual meeting, Mayo surprised the crowd with a flamboyant

demonstration of cultural pride. "Someone has suggested we should put away our beads and feathers and move on," Mayo told the gathering. "I say that we need to remember who we are. I say it's time for us maybe to put away the suit jackets and ties!" With that, he stripped off his coat and tie and put on a beaded necklace, moosehide vest, and gloves trimmed in beaver fur. "It's time maybe to put something aside, okay, but it is not our culture. It is not our pride." Then Mayo jumped over the speaker's table onto the stage where Peter John from Minto, the ninety-two-year-old traditional chief of Interior Athabascans, was seated with his wife, Elsie. Mayo began dancing and singing a celebration song from his home village of Tanana. As he sang in Koyukon, people in the audience from Interior villages joined along, cheered on by the hundreds of other Natives and observers in the convention hall.

Above: Chief Peter John of Minto is remembered for his leadership. *(Roy Corral)*

Facing page: Hazel Ambrose checks on moose meat and salmon strips in her smoke-house. *(Roy Corral)*

People of the Yukon Flats

By Velma Wallis

It is said that 10,000 years ago Gwich'in people were one of the many groups who traveled over the land bridge connecting Asia to North America. The Gwich'in arrived and settled in the flatlands. We have endured.

The Gwich'in people live the simple yet complex life based around a belief that we cannot survive without each other. All of our hunting techniques and spiritual beliefs are surrounded by this philosophy. The Gwich'in used to build huge, round fences to corral moose or caribou, which they brought down inside the fence. They worked together to do this. In some way, the Gwich'in people have always tried to stick together despite their adversities.

Before the Westerners arrived, our lives depended solely upon moose, caribou, ducks, fish, beaver, muskrats, porcupine, and other animals. We developed an almost religious attitude toward these animals, for without them our lives would be threatened. That is why we always used the word "respect," because back then without respect, we could become careless and perish.

In addition to these animals, we used other raw

Expertly cut fish hang on racks for drying. *(Roy Corral)*

Freshly killed caribou is process by women from Arctic Village. *(Karen Jettmar/AlaskaStock.com)*

materials for many different purposes. For instance we used birch bark and spruce roots to make containers to cook in or store berries in. Canoes also were made with huge pieces of birch bark bound together with young spruce roots and sealed with spruce sap. Willow and spruce were used to make fish traps, snowshoes, and bows and arrows. Tanned moose skins and furs were used for summer and winter clothing and plant-dyed porcupine quills embellished our attire.

The Gwich'in developed customs that shaped and dictated our lives. Our culture included rituals, such as dancing and religious practices and beliefs that interacted with the animals and the land.

Then came the time when the Gwich'in world changed completely. My grandmother told of the time when her band first heard that Hudson's Bay Co. fur traders had arrived on the banks of the Yukon River, in 1847, at what is now known as Fort Yukon. They had come out of Canada. She said her people were upriver, in the area of what later became known as Circle City, when one of their scouts arrived and told them about these fur traders.

My grandmother's people packed up their things and went down immediately. There they met the traders and, as time passed, my grandmother traded in her moose skin dress for one made of calico, and the hunters traded their bows and arrows for guns and powder. After contact with the Western world, many of our meaningful rituals were wiped out and remain only a dim memory in our Elders' minds.

Later when Alaska was purchased by the United States from Russia in 1867, the Canadian fur traders left Fort Yukon. The Gwich'in people continued living in the settlement, which they called *Gwichyaa Zhee*.

In the short time since, many things have happened. My grandmother's daughter Nina told me about the time she remembered when diseases arrived in our area and decimated a third of our population. She said, "At first when people died, they had funerals and people wept for their lost ones. Later, about ten times a day they carried dead people to graveyards, and people no longer cried."

But the Gwich'in people, like other Athabascans and Alaskan Natives, continued on. We have tried to keep up with the many changes brought by Western culture, some of which have made subsistence lifestyles easier. Yet others have made life more complicated, as people fall to addictions such as alcoholism.

Our town has gone through many different people, who have moved on or met their demise. We've seen a major hospital come and go. We have seen many different restaurants, stores, airlines, and even an Air Force base. Today we have commuter airlines flying to Fairbanks. We have a store, a post office, and about 600 people.

On December 17, 1971, the Alaska Native Claims Settlement Act passed into law, and the Gwich'in people begin to reclaim not only their lands, but their lives.

A young girl playing at fish camp gets tangled in a net. *(Roy Corral)*

CHIEF WILLIAM OF TANANA   PAUL WILLIAMS TANANA.   CHIEF CHARLIE OF MINTU.

A groundbreaking gathering of the Tanana Chiefs took place July 5-6, 1915, in Fairbanks. Left to right, seated: Chief Alexander of Tolovana, Chief Thomas of Nenana, Chief Evan of Coschaket, and Chief Alexander William of Tanana. Left to right, standing: Chief William of Tanana, Paul Williams of Tanana, and Chief Charlie of Minto. *(ASL-P277-004-022, Alaska State Library, Wickersham State Historic Site)*

Our people began to remember their dances, their songs, their stories. They began to retain their former strength and pride. Slowly, a sobriety movement began to spread, not only through the Yukon flatlands, but throughout Alaska. I remember a quote by one of the many sobriety counselors who passed through our area: "Without sobriety, there is no ballgame."

The one thing that has sustained through time is our dependence on animals for survival. Our lives follow the hunting season. In summer-time, the Yukon River is lined with fish wheels and fishnets and people camping along the river, drying king salmon over racks. In fall, the Gwich'in people go out in their aluminum boats with outboard motors in search of moose and ducks, for winter food.

During the winter, after their wood supply is secure and previously obtained food has been stored, the Gwich'in snare rabbits, which they eat to

supplement their diet of moose meat, dried fish, and ducks. Just as spring arrives, much to everyone's relief, the people rush to trap beaver and muskrats. As children, my siblings and I used to squabble over the muskrat tails, which we would toast on the stove until they became crispy and were just like candy to us.

In time, Fort Yukon has adjusted to the many changes, good and bad. Today we have computers, fax machines, satellite dishes, cars, planes, telephones, cable television, and much of everything else that the modern world has to offer. Yet we have remained simple in our values. The one thing that has held the Gwich'in people together through the chaos of change in the last 150 years is a deeply embedded relationship to the animals, land, and subsistence lifestyle.

We are the Gwichyaa Gwich'in, "People of the Yukon Flats."

Facing page: Seline Alexander is an expert at beadwork, as were generations before her. *(Roy Corral)*

Above: McGarrett John keeps his ears warm with a wolf-fur hat. *(Roy Corral)*

While **Velma Wallis** *is currently living in Fairbanks, her home village is Fort Yukon, which lies at the junction of the Yukon and Porcupine rivers. She is a mother of four and an award-winning author of three books:* Two Old Women (1993) *and* Bird Girl and the Man Who Followed the Sun (1996), *in which she retells Gwich'in Athabascan legends of courage and survival, and a cathartic work titled* Raising Ourselves: A Gwich'in Coming of Age Story from the Yukon River (2002).

Eyak

Traditional Homeland: **Eyak**

At the time of the Russian arrival, the Eyaks occupied the Gulf of Alaska coast between present-day Cordova and Yakutat. According to old stories, the Eyak moved out of the Interior down the Copper River to the coast. The Eyak held rich salmon fishing grounds at the mouth of the great river. But they were a relatively small group, raided and squeezed by their neighbors, particularly the Sugpiaq (formerly called Chugach Alutiiq) of Prince William Sound, who claimed some of the same territory. The Eyak were friendlier with the Tlingit people. Their social structures were similar, and intermarriages occurred frequently. But assimilation by the larger Tlingit society also contributed to the disappearance of Eyak.

The Russians traded with Eyak, sent missionaries to the area, and recognized them as a distinct culture, even in designating Eyak territory on their maps. But this was lost on the Americans. By the 1880s, Tlingit expansion had pushed the remaining Eyaks into the Copper River Delta, where about 200 Eyaks lived in two villages and several camps. The Americans arrived and started canneries,

. . . for now Krauss calls Eyak "the language of memory."

The king salmon of the Copper River are sought after by restaurateurs across the country. *(Roy Corral)*

competing with the Eyaks for salmon. They introduced alcohol, disease, and—from the Chinese cannery workers—opium. But by 1900, the sixty surviving Eyaks had congregated at an old campsite near the canneries on the west end of Eyak Lake. In 1906, this last Eyak settlement, known as Old Town, became part of the new town of Cordova, created as a railroad port terminal.

Today the Native Village of Eyak in Cordova is a federally recognized tribe with 515 enrolled members, who have ancient roots in Eyak lands.

Although the language of the Eyak band has distant links to both Athabascan and Tlingit, it started developing as a separate language about 3,500 years ago, according to noted Alaskan linguist Dr. Michael Krauss. And until January 2008, when Marie Smith Jones died at age eighty-nine, she was the only living Eyak who still spoke the language, a lonely distinction.

"I sit in front of the TV. I talk and talk to it in my language, but it don't talk back," Jones once told an interviewer. "I pray in my language, but God don't talk back in it. When the pain gets so bad, then I call him. I call him just so I can hear my language again."

The "him" is Dr. Krauss, who directed the Alaska Native Language Center in Fairbanks from its establishment in 1972 to his retirement as professor emeritus in June 2000. Krauss is a non-Native man, yet the only person in the world today who speaks Eyak. He learned the language in the 1960s when he worked with Jones and Eyak Elders Anna Nelson Harry of the Yakutat and Lena Nacktan of Cordova to record Eyak stories and write an Eyak dictionary. Some of the stories were published in 1982, titled *In Honor of Eyak: the Art of Anna Nelson Harry.* Eyak is documented as a spoken language, but for now Krauss calls it "the language of memory."

Meanwhile, an effort is underway to keep Eyak from becoming a culture of memory. Today the Eyak Preservation Council exists to protect the ancestral lands and resources of the Eyak. Led by a handful of Eyak descendants and their allies, the group and its efforts have gained notice by the nation's media. Founder and president

Faye Pahl's Eyak name is "Tanakamaa," which means "eggs from the fish." She was born after her mother ate a meal of fish eggs. *(Roy Corral)*

Facing page: An aerial view of Eyak Lake near Cordova. *(Jim Wark/AlaskaStock.com)*

Dune Lankard was once named a "Hero of the Planet" by *Time* magazine. Joined by Pam Smith, who leads the Council's efforts on cultural preservation and language program, Lankard and others are trying to revive their culture, learning what it means to be Eyak.

Much of what is known about the Eyak comes from interviews and fieldwork conducted by Frederica de Laguna and Kaj Birket-Smith, published as *The Eyak Indians of the Copper River Delta, Alaska* (1933). Krauss's work in the 1960s provided additional insights, in part through Anna Nelson Harry's masterful storytelling.

The late Marie Smith Jones was twelve years old in 1930 and already working in the canneries, when young anthropologist de Laguna arrived in Cordova. The U.S. Marshal directed de Laguna to the local Natives. De Laguna soon realized the Eyak language was unique and through her work, Eyaks gained a place in the literature as the most recently recognized Alaskan Native group. At age sevetyeight, Jones remembered watching de Laguna and her associates interviewing her favorite uncle.

"I pretended I was fishing from the beach," she said, "but I was watching them. I didn't want them to hurt him."

Jones had grown up in a two-room cabin on Eyak Lake with her sister and parents, Scar and Minnie Stevens, who worked for the railroad and salmon canneries. Although she was forbidden to speak the language of the government-run school in Cordova, she and her family conversed in Eyak at home. Her mother was devout Russian Orthodox, and raised Marie in Native ways as well as those of the church. Her parents fished the salmon runs, taking her in the boat when she was four days old; they preserved berries in seal oil; her father showed her how to hunt and live off the land. As a baby, she couldn't stomach milk; her mother chewed up fish and other foods to feed her. She remembered her mother getting help from a medicine woman once, and her parents told about Jones's maternal grandfather, a shaman who used to go into a trance, balancing flat on a string strung across the living room.

Jones emerged as something of an activist.

Western sandpipers and dunlins feeding at Hartney Bay, Cordova. *(Jim R. Kohl/ AlaskaStock.com)*

Beginning her work among the Eyak people in 1930, pioneering anthropologist de Laguna would spend the following years documenting Alaska's early Native people. Jones, meantime, would stay in Cordova through four marriages and a long battle with alcoholism. She quit drinking in 1970 and moved to Anchorage three years later. In 1992, her sister Sophie died, leaving Jones as the last Native speaker of the Eyak language. As an old woman, she would bring to mind phone calls to Sophie and conferring on the meaning of an elusive Eyak word. Together, they would remember.

Jones emerged in her last decades of life as something of an activist. She spoke against logging ancestral Eyak lands and participated in a lawsuit to stop clear-cutting by the Eyak Corp., a village corporation out of Cordova made up primarily of Sugpiaq (Chugach Alutiiq) and Tlingits. She worked to fund a scholarship for Indian youth at the University of Alaska Fairbanks. She spoke with

Each spring, Cordova hosts a festival celebrating the migrating birds. Shown here are western sandpipers and dunlins. *(Roy Corral)*

Facing page: Dune Lankard has been a strong voice among his people, an environmental activist as well as an advocate to keep the Eyak language and traditions alive. *(Roy Corral)*

The late Honorary Chief Marie Smith Jones was the last Native speaker of Eyak language.
(Roy Corral)

assurance that God had been preparing her to be the last speaker of the Eyak language.

"I know I'm supposed to lead my people," she said.

As Eyak Chief, Jones retold her people's story at intertribal gatherings in the Lower 48 and carried the Eyak banner with her son, William, in the Alaska leg of the International Peace and Dignity Journey of Indigenous People.

In 1995, Jones and de Laguna met again in Cordova for the first Eyak potlatch in eighty years. Dr. Krauss came also, greeting Jones in an outpouring of Eyak. The event was videotaped for a documentary titled *More Than Words*. The potlatch celebrated reburial a year earlier of an unnamed Eyak man, whose bones had been held by the Smithsonian Institution since 1917. As Chief, Jones was to lead and she was nervous, afraid she would make a mistake. About two dozen people gathered in the mist at the burial site for a brief healing ceremony, then adjourned to an empty warehouse for feasting, dancing, and gift exchanges. Jones brought the celebration full circle by bestowing Eyak names to the young people. She chuckled at the name she chose for Lankard, an outspoken critic of logging Eyak lands. His Eyak name, *Jamachakih*, means "little bird that never stops chirping." Said Jones, "He was a little chatterbox when he was young."

Later during the celebration, de Laguna herself reflected on the historic potlatch, "It's a rebirth of a people . . . The hope is in the children, who come to feel pride in being Eyak. We don't know the form Eyak culture will take in the future but it will always be distinctly Eyak."

A mingling of cultures occurred at Katalla, where the Tlingit people dwelt from prehistoric times and the Eyak later settled. This photo dating from 1907–09 depicts a Katalla-area girl wearing traditional garb, including a nose labret. *(Alaska State Library, Ray W. Moss Photograph Collection)*

Tlingit

Traditional
Homelands:
Tlingit

The islands, seaways, and rain forests of Southeast Alaska create a dramatic landscape, a place mysterious and awesome in scale and complexity. Jagged, snowcapped peaks reach skyward, sometimes bathed by sunlight, often shrouded in fog and mist. Dense stands of cedar and spruce skirt the mountains in varying shades of gray, blue, and green. The air resonates with the white noise of water cascading off the mountainsides, of streams seen and unseen coursing downhill into low-lying bogs and wetlands. Fjords gouged by ancient glaciers warp the coastline in a labyrinth of watery passages. Eagles and ravens soar overhead. Bear and wolf shadow the shore.

This is home to the Tlingit people, whose culture is as complex and dramatic as the land they inhabit. Tlingit art is bold—the massive totem poles, intricate weaving, flamboyant headdresses—these and other visual expressions of the Tlingit culture are emblazoned with stylized designs that depict animals and humans. More than mere decorations, these designs are important crests. They signify ownership, relationships, and family histories, and are

More than mere decorations, these designs are important crests.

Facing page: Albert Paddy of Klukwan motors to check his subsistence nets on the Chilkat River. *(Roy Corral)*

133

The Chilkat River wends through the northern reaches of the Southeast Panhandle. *(Roy Corral)*

accompanied by stories that explain their origin, often connected with a legendary ancestor. Crests speak to a less visible but unifying—and complicated—aspect of Tlingit culture: its social organization.

To start with, Tlingit society is divided into two parts, or moieties: Eagle and Raven. Relationships are traced through the mother's family. A person is either Eagle or Raven, the same as his or her mother. Traditionally, marriages were between people of opposite moieties, but this practice isn't strictly observed today. The moieties are further divided into many families, or clans, each identified by their crests. Each moiety has more than a dozen different known clans today. Some of the Raven clan include Frog, Coho Salmon, Swan; those of the Eagle include Killer Whale, Shark, and Bear, to name only a few. This determines how the Tlingit are related to one another, past and present. Tlingit people can follow their heritage through bloodlines, home territories, and ancestral clan houses. People in the

same moiety may refer to each other as brothers and sisters, whether
or not they are blood kin. In old Tlingit tradition, children were
taught life skills by their maternal uncles.

"Basically, everyone is related in the community. We're all family,
either through blood relations or through tribal ways," explained
Mike A. Jackson, a Tlingit from Kake.

This has all sorts of implications: What one person does affects
the entire community. Younger people take care of the older people,
who in turn teach them. If someone does something good or helps in
some way, they are to be repaid with gifts or services of equal value.
In the Tlingit way, people are taught to relate to one another with
respect, rather than disrespect.

"My generation and the people who learn from Elders pass
these things onto our children. . . . We incorporate these values
with Western-style living. We walk on both sides," said Jackson.
As a magistrate, Jackson was instrumental in helping form Kake's
restorative justice circle that encourages peacemaking and living well,

Bold color, clan symbols, and detailed button work are hallmarks of Tlingit robes. *(Roy Corral)*

Early Tlingits repeatedly resisted intrusions into their territory.

Ketchikan's Totem Heritage Center includes displays of 19th-century totem poles that were recovered from various sites throughout Southeast, along with replicas and other modern works. In fall, winter, and spring, traditional carvers are on hand to teach seminars and work-shops. (*Tricia Brown*)

protecting young people, and celebrating what he calls "the good side of Kake."

"We shouldn't lose the values we are born with. We need to hold on to our identity. It makes a solid foundation to know who we are, to accept it, work with it and pass it on."

Nearly 14,000 Tlingit live in Alaska, most in Southeast's seaside towns and villages, such as Kake on Kupreanof Island. They are, by far, the largest Native group in Southeast. Tlingit ancestors may have lived on these same shores as long as 9,000 years ago, the age of the earliest known campsites; these early people probably depended on maritime resources and used boats, since their midden piles held bones of fish off the ocean bottom. Later sites, 4,000 and 3,000 years old, show more direct links with Tlingit-styled stone tools.

The temperate coastal environment of Southeast provided abundant resources, and Tlingit culture flourished. Prior to contact with outsiders and the diseases they brought, there may have been as many as 20,000 Tlingit living on the bays and inlets along Alaska's Southeast coast, suggests Wallace M. Olson in *The Tlingit* (1991), a comprehensive introduction to Tlingit culture and history. Other important works about Tlingit culture include a series of books edited by Nora and Richard Dauenhauer with interviews, oral histories, biographies, and life stories collected from contemporary Tlingits, and writings by anthropologist Frederica de Laguna, which draw from extensive fieldwork in Tlingit country.

The early Tlingits repeatedly resisted intrusions into their territory. They battled the Russians numerous times at different locations, including Yakutat and Sitka. Five years after Alaska became a U.S. possession, when it was still a military district, a U.S. Navy warship shelled and burned the Native village of Angoon in a confrontation that more than a century later remains a tragic page in American history. At the turn of the century, the Tlingit people were squeezed off their traditional fishing, hunting, and village sites by American gold miners, cannery operators, and the federal government's new Tongass National Forest. Tlingit leaders decided in

Tlingit dancer Ernie Bernhardt. (Roy Corral)

1912 that the clans needed to unite to claim their rights, and formed the Alaska Native Brotherhood and several years later, the Alaska Native Sisterhood. With the passage in 1924 of the citizenship act for Indians and Eskimos, Tlingits increased their political force. Tlingit William Paul was elected to the territorial Legislature that year, the first Alaska Native to be elected. In the mid-1930s the Tlingit joined with the Haida people to press the first Native land claims lawsuit in Alaska against the federal government.

The Tlingit sense of ownership remains strong; they value the ethic of fairness. Dances, songs, stories, and clan crests are possessions of individuals and clans. A source of irritation among some Tlingit today is what they see as disrespect from visitors to take pictures, make tape recordings, or copy crest designs without permission.

Subsistence fishermen from the village of Klawock balance precariously as they haul in a net full of salmon.
(Roy Corral)

The Tlingit are recognized for many remarkable visual expressions of their culture. They are noted woodworkers and weavers. For their winter villages, they historically built huge clan houses out of cedar planks, with sleeping areas inside that were screened off with elaborately carved panels. Similar clan houses today are built for community gatherings. The people also carved great oceangoing canoes from massive logs. They

carved totem poles to tell stories and histories, to mark a grave, or remember a great person. Often, the carver was commissioned by a member of the opposite moiety.

Totem poles are still carved today, and commissioned works by master carvers can command thousands of dollars for non-Native art collectors or museums. However, for most artists, carving a pole for a clan member or institution within their culture remains most satisfying. As tradition dictates, when the completed pole is raised, the carver tells what the design signifies, the story of the pole. The poles owner pays the carver and all those who helped, often by hosting a potlatch party.

Weaving continues today as well, although not to the degree of past centuries when most clothing, baskets, and other practical and ceremonial items were woven from cedar bark, wool, roots, and strips of fur. Often at potlatches in the past, robes that might have taken months or years to weave would be snipped apart and given away in a show of wealth. A dedicated group of contemporary weavers is hard at work in Southeast today to keep the art going. They are working individually and in collaboration to rebuild a cultural inventory. They have completed several large pieces of ceremonial regalia, such as Chilkat and Raven's Tail robes, which are brought out for special occasions such as Celebration, a festival held in Juneau in even-

Tlingit and Haida weathered pole rests in covered storage. Contemporary carvers such as Nathan Jackson are commissioned to copy aging poles, following traditional forms and similar carving methods as their ancestors. Jackson jokes, however, about using a chainsaw to help make the first rough cuts, a luxury his ancestors never imagined. (Tricia Brown)

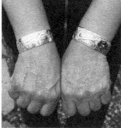

Thunderbird and Whale originally stood in the old village of Klinkwan on Prince of Wales Island. A copy by Haida carver John Wallace was created during the 1930s. Tlingit carver Nathan Jackson was commissioned to carve a second copy when Wallace's began to degrade. *(Tricia Brown)*

Bottom: Tlingit silversmiths often etch clan images on bracelets and other fine silver pieces. *(Tricia Brown)*

numbered years. Traditionally, only men carved and women wove, but now a few women are carving and a few men are learning to weave.

The Tlingit share cultural similarities with the Haida and Tsimshian, but each language is unique. The Tlingit share distinct linguistic similarities in verb structures to the Athabascans, clues that the two cultures were linked long ago at some point in the Na-Dene Indian migration. Tlingit lore tells of how the people came to the coast, some under the glacier, from the Interior. A group of Tlingits moved to inland Canada from the coast during early contact with traders.

Few people younger than forty are fluent in Tlingit today, though there are numerous attempts to rekindle use of the language. As in Alaska's other Native cultures, many things important to the culture have no equivalent in English, so maintaining the language is seen by many as vital to maintaining the culture. Village schools teach the Tlingit language in classes, and the Sealaska Heritage Institute, the nonprofit arm of Sealaska Regional Corp., created funding for language-immersion retreats. Online resources allow students of any age to view and listen to word lists, phrases, and stories.

In Sitka, Pauline Duncan developed her own approach as a first-grade teacher, teaching the language by using Tlingit words throughout the day. Classroom rules were given in Tlingit, and the children exchanged greetings in the morning and afternoon in Tlingit. When they studied rocks and minerals or insects, they learned the names in Tlingit as well as English. They even said the pledge to the flag in Tlingit. Although Pauline is Tlingit and heard the language as a child in Angoon, she never learned to speak it because she was away at boarding school. She started teaching Tlingit in her class several years ago, partly as a way to learn. Her husband Albert, a fluent speaker who grew up in a fish camp on Excursion Inlet, helped her with vocabulary and grammar. She also visited regularly with Tlingit Elders in Sitka. Along with the language, she taught about other aspects of the culture, bringing in Native foods for the kids to try, and inviting Elders in to tell stories. Even the children in her class who came from other cultural backgrounds benefit, she said.

"The Tlingit culture is of this area, a part of the history," Duncan said. "It's building the foundations so they can extend what they're learning about the Tlingit to cultures they may encounter later in life. They'll know that wherever they live, there is a local culture, with language, dance, customs, and stories."

Now Pauline and Albert Duncan's Tlingit curriculum resources are made available for all teachers (and students) through the Alaska Native Knowledge Network, a Web site for expanding and sharing Alaska Native traditional knowledge, history, stories, languages, science, religion, and more.

Joe Hotch of Klukwan's Eagle moiety dons full traditional regalia. The Killer Whale hat in his hands was carved more than a century ago.
(Roy Corral)

Carving Traditions

By Nathan Jackson

As a young person, I was asked to practice Native dancing for the Fourth of July. We spent some time with all of the Elders, learning some songs and how to dance. I did not take that much interest in it, because it took me away from my buddies. But then I found out that my buddies weren't doing anything that exciting anyway. So I danced on a flatbed truck in the Fourth of July parade. My grandfather felt it would be better for me to try and learn the old ways, and my feeling was that at the time I wanted to learn the easier way.

During the winter months as a teenager, I spent a lot of time cutting wood and watching my uncle, Ted Laurence, carve small totem poles. He asked me to try a small totem pole about four inches high. It wasn't too bad, but I didn't think I wanted to continue carving. Since my grandfather was teaching me how to fish, I wanted to be a fisherman.

After serving in the Army, I came back to Southeast, where I fished and looked for odd jobs, which wasn't too successful. In 1962, I ended up in the hospital at Mount Edgecumbe in Sitka, because they thought I had tuberculosis. Through occupational therapy, a lot of yellow cedar was available, so I filled up the whole showcase with small poles. After a couple of months I was released, and I ended up dancing with the Chilkat Dancers in Haines. Some carvers in Haines were working at Alaska Indian Arts, Inc., and there I met Leo Jacobs, who did miniature poles. I also have another uncle, Horace Marks, who had carved. I felt that I could be able to make a living at carving, rather than trying to be a fisherman.

During this time, I also took an interest in doing portraits. That fall, I was accepted to the Institute of American Indian Arts in Santa Fe, New Mexico, where I spent two years. Then the opportunity came to go with Alaska Indian Arts to the 1964 World's Fair in New York. It gave me an opportunity to look at and study some of the Tlingit art at the various museums in New York. Later, back in Haines, I worked as an instructor for the Alaska Indian Arts. I met Bill Holm, an authority on Northwest Coast Indian arts from Seattle, who pointed out a

Nathan Jackson works in a carving shed near Saxman Totem Park, outside Ketchikan. *(Roy Corral)*

lot of elements in flat design during a class he was teaching in Haines. It enlightened my understanding of two-dimensional Native design. I inquired from Bill, on the side, about the adzing techniques used on the old poles and spent a lot of time practicing and making my own tools. From Bill, I've gotten a lot of referrals for jobs, which helped launch my career.

I spend much time looking at art pieces in museums and studying those pieces. Drawing, at least for me, is pretty important to come up with a likeness of any Indian art pieces. You have to be to see what you're looking at, and you have to be able to critique your own work. In totem pole work, at least in Southeast Alaska, there are three different styles—Tsimshian, Haida, and Tlingit—so you have to be able to distinguish the differences and try to overlap. The Haidas used large red cedar, bigger in diameter than the Tsimshian and Tlingit poles. The eyes on each figure were fairly large, and there was a lot of interconnecting with the various figures. The Tsimshian from the upper Skeena River in British Columbia used longer trees. Tsimshian figures are more rounded and realistic than the Haida, and the eyes are not as large in proportion to the face. The Tlingit style is closer to the Tsimshian than the Haida, with rounded-off figures and fairly deep carving. The main difference between the Tlingit and the Tsimshian is the treatment of the face. In doing reproductions, I've had to do the Haida style, and in doing research, I've made a lot of interesting discoveries.

In my original work, I basically tried to maintain the traditional Tlingit style in such things as masks, totem poles, etc. There have been a few exceptions, such as an eagle in Ketchikan called Thundering Wings. In our language this is called Kitch-xan: Kitch meaning "wings," and xan meaning "sound of thunder." This piece is a fairly realistic representation of an eagle, with Tlingit elements in the wing designs, tail, and treatment of the head. The only completely nontraditional carving I have done was two sets of doors, carved in the low relief, for a church in Ketchikan. The subject matter is from the Hebrew Scriptures.

I enjoy doing artwork that has been commissioned by my own people, such as the headdresses and masks, because they won't be sitting on a wall, but they'll be used. It probably means more to me to be recognized by my people. I've been commissioned to do both wood carving and jewelry. Generally I prefer working on bigger projects, such as totem poles, large screens, and canoes.

Over the years, I've had jobs that required, in the contract, that I take apprentices. I also have had

Cruise-ship passengers to Ketchikan can make a trip to nearby Saxman Totem Park, where they are invited to view carvers at work. Here, Nathan Jackson was on hand for a brief visit. *(Tricia Brown)*

people ask to apprentice with me. And then there was my son Stephen, who was probably my best apprentice yet. A prerequisite for an apprentice is desire to learn to carve, a little drawing ability, and possibly artists in the family background. I get them started on making or buying their own tools.

At one time after I came to Ketchikan, someone referred to me as "Nathan Jackson, the last of the Tlingit carvers." I had a pretty negative reaction to this because I felt there were many more carvers on the horizon, given the opportunity. This is one reason why I took them on. Eventually, most apprentices launch off on their own and develop their own styles. Many of them have been fairly successful in making a living from carving.

My son is a better carver than his father, but he's moving into a different direction. The school I went to in Santa Fe, New Mexico, would relish having Stephen as a student because he's more experimental and expanding out and so on.

One of the misconceptions that some people have about

Totem poles in Klawock, Prince of Wales Island. *(Mark Kelley/ AlaskaStock.com)*

unpaid debts. Usually the tallest poles would show rank and nobility, and so in the olden days when a canoe full of people would come to a village, they would know which house to go to first.

Sometimes I kind of feel like a trailblazer who has looked over an old trail covered with brush that needed to be cleared away, so the trail could be reestablished. Through digging and looking at old works, I wonder what a lot of the old-time master carvers went through and how they were dedicated to their work. I appreciate being able to try to copy, or reproduce, some of the older works. I feel fortunate that I've been able to receive large commissions and make a living as an artist, and I've been able to watch others follow and also be successful. I can see a lot of good carvers on the horizon, and this makes me want to forge ahead, to continue to improve.

the art is that totem poles were worshipped. That's not true. In the olden days, the poles would reflect different stories relating to a particular clan. Since there was no written language, it was a way to remind the Elders to tell the young people about their heritage by what the totem poles meant. Some were stories of heroism and morals, and then some were about

Adze in hand, Nathan Jackson explains that his toolbox includes custom-made and store bought tools. *(Tricia Brown)*

Tlingit master carver **Nathan Jackson** *and his wife Dorica live south of Saxman, near Ketchikan. His commissioned carvings may be found in museums and private collections all around the world. The carvings are equally far ranging in scope, from a traditional cedar dugout canoe, house posts, masks, original totem poles, and copies of historic poles. Together with his son Stephen, Jackson has traveled extensively; the father-son duo has carved in Washington, D.C., England, Australia, Switzerland, Germany, and Belgium. While Nathan's work is steeped in tradition, he applauds his son's expansion into contemporary forms using mixed media.*

In Alaska, Nathan Jackson's work has been installed at the Museum of the North in Fairbanks, the Anchorage Museum at Rasmuson Center, the Totem Heritage Center in Ketchikan, and the Alaska State Museum in Juneau, as well as numerous other venues. Many of the replica poles at Totem Bight State Historical Park, outside Ketchikan, were carved by Jackson.

Among his numerous awards, Jackson was designated a "living cultural treasure" in 1995, receiving a National Heritage Fellowship from the National Endowment for the Arts. Later, he was pictured in his Raven regalia on a U.S. postage stamp set that featured American Indian dances. And when the National Museum of the American Indian opened in Washington, D.C., in September 2004, Jackson was honored for his outstanding artistry and representation of Tlingit heritage. He holds an honorary doctorate of humanities degree, awarded by the University of Alaska Southeast.

Tsimshian

Traditional
Homelands:
Tsimshian

For four days they feasted. The Raven clan presented salmon on the first day. The Killer whale clan served halibut on the second. The Wolf clan prepared deer for the third. And on the fourth day, the Eagle clan hosted with every traditional Tsimshian food imaginable—fish eggs, hooligan, seaweed, clams, cockles, abalone, crab, fry bread, blueberries, salmonberries, "half-dried" fish that had been smoked over alder then steamed. For four days the Tsimshian Indians of Metlakatla and their guests feasted, danced, sang, and celebrated the raising of three newly carved totem poles.

"It was the neatest thing that ever happened," recalled Metlakatla resident Theo McIntyre.

For nearly 100 years, that Tsimshian of Metlakatla, on Annette Island in Southeast Alaska, were separated from the most visible of their Indian traditions—carving, singing, dancing, and potlatching. The founders of "New Metlakatla" chose to adopt the "white man's ways," the people say, when they left their Tsimshian villages in British Columbia to join Anglican preacher William Duncan.

About 800 Tsimshian people followed Duncan to Alaska.

From left, Carla Schleusner, Chris Leask, and Melody Leask in their dance finery.
(Roy Corral)

Missionary Duncan persuaded a group of Tsimshians to create a model community, to escape the damaging influences of alcohol and disease brought by visitors on steamships through Canada. In 1887, about 800 Tsimshian people followed Duncan to Alaska, to the site of a former Tlingit village on Annette Island. Here they built the new town of Metlakatla. In 1891, Duncan obtained reservation status for the 86,000-acre island from the U.S. government. Today it is the only federally recognized Indian reservation in Alaska.

People still worship in the faith that Duncan preached, although the town now has churches of four other denominations. Although Duncan appreciated Tsimshian art—he had four totem poles inside his original church in British Columbia—he encouraged

From the top of Yellow Hill, Metlakatla's place along the water is visible. *(Don Pitcher/ AlaskaStock.com)*

people to use their time in more economically productive ways, and artistic expressions withered among Metlakatlans. He did, however, learn and encourage use of the language, which apparently thrived until the government schoolteachers arrived in the early 1900s with their English-only mandate.

The Sealaska Heritage Institute, the nonprofit arm of the Sealaska Regional Corp., estimates there are about thirty speakers in Alaska and another 300 in Canada. The Institute periodically offers two-week intensive workshops each year, and directs those interested in formal instruction to contact British Columbia institutions that offer courses. Sealaska continues to expand its Web site resources with a bilingual dictionary for Tsimshian, Haida, and Tlingit languages.

Top: Members of the Metlakatla Choral Society gathered for a formal portrait in the early days of New Metlakatla. *(Alaska State Library, Alaska Lantern Slides Collection)*

In 2010, there were 1,405 people living in Metlakatla, 82 percent of whom were Alaska Native. Accessible only by air and water, modern Metlakatla has a salmon hatchery, a cold-storage facility, tribal court system, and several small businesses including a meat market, grocery, hardware store, and hotel. By air, the island is about fifteen minutes south of Ketchikan; it's an hour by ferry. The community regulates who can live and work there, requiring permits and local sponsors for outsiders who want to stay any length of time.

Commercial fishing is a mainstay, and the community is developing its tourism potential, as the state ferry serves Metlakatla from spring through fall. Recent efforts include a partnership with one of the commercial fishing captains made famous through Discovery Channel's popular broadcast, *Deadliest Catch*. David Lethin retrofitted his ship in 2007 to accommodate 150 spectators who can come along and watch (and stay out of the way) while the

Annette Island is one of the warmest, rainiest places in the state. *(Roy Corral)*

107-foot *Aleutian Ballad* works the fishing grounds off Annette Island. A portion of every ticket sold goes to the Metlakatla Indian Community.

Other visitors to Metlakatla can tour the town, including Duncan's cottage and museum, the original church, and the historic 1918 cannery, then stop at the longhouse for pit-baked salmon, traditional dancing, and visits with Tsimshian artists who have rediscovered the ancient ways nearly lost to them.

"We almost completely adopted the culture of the white man, and we've done real good with it. Now we are just getting back into our own," said Jack Hudson, a highly respected Tsimshian master carver and a member of the Wolf clan. Hudson reintroduced carving to the Metlakatla Tsimshian in 1974, when he came home for a visit and ended up staying. He'd been living at the time in Washington state, studying old Tsimshian works in museums and carving under the tutelage of Northwest Coast Indian art expert Bill Holm.

For decades Hudson in turn taught students at the Metlakatla high school, demonstrating carving and other aspects of traditional Tsimshian art. When the students completed his program, they could create and connect the seven elements

Artist Wayne Hewson paints a stylized design on his yellow cedar carving of a salmon. *(Roy Corral)*

of Tsimshian design into human and animal figures in drawing, painting, and carving. Each student also made eight carving knives and an adze, tools crucial to the art. The knife metal came from old bandsaws from the community's sawmill; adzes were made from old car springs. Hudson, an internationally recognized artist, figured each student came out of the program with a personally tailored set of tools worth about $500.

Fishing, hunting, and gathering beach foods today remain the strongest link to ancestral Tsimshian ways. The local store brings convenience, but nothing replaces the locally harvested foods found in every freezer and cupboard. Tiny buildings all around town are smokehouses used to dry fish and seaweed. In addition to seafood and edible plants and berries, people hunt deer that live on the island. Wayne Hewson, a well-known Tsimshian artist and carver, likes to eat deer and also uses hooves for making dance rattles. His freezer is crammed with deer legs dropped off by friends after hunting trips.

In 1996, Hewson took on a major art project—painting Tsimshian designs on the community longhouse, part of a larger effort to get Metlakatla ready for tourists after its leaders decided to tap into the lucrative cruise-ship market. Hewson also is a friend and

"We're very proud of this community."

protégé of David Boxley, the first Alaskan Tsimshian carver to achieve national prominence. Boxley has carved more than sixty-five totem poles since 1980, including a couple in his birthplace of Metlakata. In addition, he helped bring back the practice of potlatching, along with all of its positive cultural aspects, including honoring the Elders, remembering the dead, adopting and giving names, feasting on traditional foods, and dancing.

About the same time that carving was introduced to Metlakatla, Boxley was instrumental in reintroducing dancing. In the 1970s several local people visited the Tsimshian in British Columbia to learn songs and movements to teach Metlakatla children as part of the federally funded Johnson O'Malley Indian Education program. The school program was so successful that, with Boxley's help,

Adorned in timeless regalia, Paul Brendible leads the dancers. *(Roy Corral*

parents of those dancing youths started the community group called Fourth Generation Dancers, their name a reminder that they were the fourth-generation descendants of the town's founders.

"Our great-grandfathers were raised through the church," said Theo McIntyre. "None of the traditional carvings or the dancing was done here. We're not blaming. [Duncan] did good. We're very proud of this community."

In the early years of the Fourth Generation Dancers, several people— among them Boxley, Barbara Fawcett, and Melody Leask—wrote many of the songs that the group performed. "Our Song" told the history of Metlakatla. Another dance called "*Whywah*" (Tsimshian for "Let's go!") came from Metlakatla crowds yelling "*Whywah!*"

at basketball games; this song is used to invite audience members to dance. The group also performed "Eagle, Drop Me a Feather," written by McIntyre's daughter, Marcella, when she was twelve. The girl was inspired by the sight of her mother looking for eagle feathers on the beach and thanking the eagle when she found one. In the dance, Eagle clan members stand in the center with feathers, calling "*shkeek*" (Eagle) to the sky. In the course of the dance, they drop their feathers to the dancers in the outer circle, who say "*gom golth wan*" (thank you).

"It's living proof that we are making a difference with our young people," said McIntyre. "It gives them more pride in who they are. When I was growing up, I went to Indian boarding school

The Four Clans totem pole in Metlakatla was carved by David Boxley. *(Roy Corral)*

in Lawrence, Kansas. The young people there would put on their traditional regalia and dance. For the few of us from Metlakatla, we wished we had something like that. . . well, now I have and it will be handed down to my children, my grandchildren."

In 2012, the dance group celebrated its 25th anniversary, and new generations are continuing to learn the songs and dances of their cultural rebirth.

Haida

Traditional Homelands: Haida

Today in Alaska, the Haida Indians are often linked to the Tlingit. The Tlingit–Haida Central Council oversees Native land allotments in Southeast; the Tlingit–Haida Housing Authority handles government-funded housing projects; the Tlingit–Haida Dancers at Anchorage perform traditional songs and ceremonies in the state's largest Native village. The Haida and the Tlingit, along with the Tsimshian people, do share cultural similarities, as well as with several other groups of indigenous people in the temperate rain forest along the Northwest Pacific Coast. They express themselves artistically through carving, painting, and weaving in a style categorically referred to as Northwest Coast Indian art, and their societies are traditionally structured around complex relationships defined by kinships through their mother's families.

But the Haida are a distinct and separate group of people, with their own language, history, and legends. Some people think the Haida language may stem from the same source as Tlingit, Eyak, and Athabascan. Linguists at the Alaska Native Language Center

The Haida ancient origins [are] something of a mystery.

Bright colors, buttons, and especially clan emblems identify the regalia of the Haida people. *(Jeff Schultz/ AlaskaStock.com)*

in Fairbanks, however, see no connection between Haida and other known languages; they consider the Haida language an "isolate." This makes the Haida ancient origins something of a mystery.

Today about 1,800 Americans report Haida ancestry, with about 4,000 more specifying Haida roots mixed with other tribal groups. Only about 425 are still living in the two remaining Alaskan villages— Hydaburg and Kasaan.

Hydaburg, a quiet village at the end of a gravel road south of Craig on Prince of Wales Island, is the primary Haida community in Alaska, although Klawock, Craig, and Ketchikan have sizable Haida populations. British Columbia remains the Haida cultural center, with a large community in Masset, on Graham Island. Visiting regularly takes place between the Alaskan and Canadian Haidas.

At age eighty-three, Kake resident Mona Frank Jackson remembered her early childhood in Masset where she lived with her grandparents in a clan house. The clan house was "one big room, like a warehouse," she recalled. She slept with her grandparents on a big feather bed surrounded by "copperhead trunks." Her grandfather got up first every morning to make coffee on a big woodstove. Three uncles also lived in the house. One made boats in the community boathouse; another was an accomplished piano player; the third was a reader in the Episcopal Church. The family would pick berries, fish, and garden.

She moved to Hydaburg in 1923 at age ten to join her mother who had remarried. It was a difficult adjustment. She was timid and scared of white people and she spoke no English, which was the only

Historically, the Haida people have been known for carving and using massive canoes as transportation across great distances, such as when a portion of the Haida Gwaii population left Canada for Alaska during the 1700s, traveling north.
(Clark James Mishler/ AlaskaStock.com)

Facing page: Kasaan's Whale House has been restored.
(Elizabeth Manfred/DCRA)

language allowed in the Hydaburg school. In the fourth grade, she was sent to the Sheldon Jackson boarding school in Sitka. She made infrequent visits to Hydaburg to see her mother. On one visit home, the family, including her grandmother traveled in a traditional dugout canoe. Her grandmother pointed to a young man on the beach. "That's the man you'll marry," she said. Later as a schoolteacher, Jackson took her first job in Kake. The school board president who met her at the steamship was the boy from the beach; true to her grandmother's prediction, they married.

The Haida's aboriginal homeland is Haida Gwaii, also known as Canada's Queen Charlotte Islands, an archipelago of two large islands and 150 smaller ones. Sometime in the 1700s, a group of Haida from the storm-lashed shore of Graham Island, largest of the islands, abandoned their villages and came to Alaska. They paddled their long, graceful cedar canoes across thirty miles of ocean to Prince of Wales, Dall, Long, and Sukkwan islands in Southeast.

The Haidas in Alaska, often called "Kaigani" after an early village, name themselves *Kiis Haade*, the "separate island people." They chose winter village sites on protected waters with sloping shores for landing their canoes. The Alaska rain forests were similar, but lacked cedar trees as massive and tall as those they left behind. They had access to most of the same seafood and sea mammals, including halibut, cod, eels, sea lions, sea otters, mussels, clams, crabs, and octopus. The new territory also had deer, wolf, mink, and beaver, animals absent in their southerly homeland.

They kept track of the year by seasonal activity. For instance, June was "Great Month," or *Qong qons*, when the people filled many canoes and sang ceremonial songs as they paddled to bird rookeries to gather eggs; some were preserved in eulachon grease for winter. Grease from eulachon, smeltlike fish, came in trade from Tsimshian on the British Columbia mainland and was highly valued as a preservative for its flavoring and delicacy. During *San gias,* the "Killer Whale Month" (July), women and children hiked into the mountains to gather cedar bark; the sound of ripping bark from the tree was likened to a killer whale blowing. The Haida built cedar-plank houses, where their extended families lived, and they carved totem poles to tell family histories or myths, and to hold the remains of the dead. To commission others to build a house or carve a totem required payment for services with elaborate potlatches.

By the time Spaniard Juan Perez sighted the Queen Charlottes in 1774, the Haida were already well established in Alaska. Englishman George Dixon first traded sea otter pelts with the people in 1787, triggering a steady summer fleet of fur traders. The Haida, he noted, had an elaborate and sophisticated material culture; they prized iron in trade to make adzes, which increased their carving efficiency. The Haida also started producing carvings from argillite (black shale) and made spruce-root baskets and hats for trade souvenirs.

By the late 1800s, the Haida adopted Christianity. They'd mostly

Facing page: Hydaburg's historical Totem Park expresses the legacy of Haida carvers. Nearly 400 people live in Hydaburg, the fourth-largest community on Prince of Wales Island. (Don Pitcher/ AlaskaStock.com)

Below: Then and now: contemporary Haida carvers fashioned a seaworthy canoe using the methods of their forefathers. Paddling toward these commercial fishing vessels, the size of the canoe and the paddlers are placed in perspective. (Clark James Mishler/ AlaskaStock.com)

A stand of young timber just outside the Kasaan Totem Village.
(Robert Spencer Ingman)

Below: Dramatic light heightens the beauty of Kasaan Bay on Prince of Wales Island.
(Robert Spencer Ingman)

replaced their cedar-bark and skin clothing with Western dress. By this time, the Alaska Haida had five permanent winter villages: Koiandlas and Howkan on Long Island; Sukkwan on Sukkwan Island; and Klinkwan and Kasaan on Prince of Wales. In 1884, with passage of the Organic Act that established a civil government in Alaska, Howkan and Klinkwan got government schools. In 1900, modern two-story houses started appearing on ruins of the communal houses in Howkan and Klinkwan. Totem poles cut down in Klinkwan appeared as supports for a new boardwalk built along the beachfront. In 1902, the people of Kasaan were promised jobs if they moved to the site of the new copper mine at New Kasaan, where they lived until the operation closed, then moved to Ketchikan in the 1940s and 1950s. In 1912, many people from the other villages moved to a new village, Hydaburg, to get a new government school.

Clara Natkong was eighty-seven when she shared the story of her family's move from Howkan to Hydaburg. Even though she was only

The Craig boat harbor
is the home of the Prince
of Wales fishing fleet.
(Robert Spencer Ingman)

three when they moved, she remembered her father, who was raised
by his mother's brother in the traditional way, telling stories and
teaching songs. As an Elder, Natkong was retelling the stories to the
children of Hydaburg.

"An important part of passing on our culture is telling stories,"
she said. "We have many, many stories, all kinds of stories. Hearing
them now I remember them." Starting in the 1970s she taught Haida
language in the school; decades later, a Haida language and culture
program was continuing in the school, but the children were coming
to Natkong's house for stories so she wouldn't have to walk up the hill
to the school. "Quite a few here can talk in Haida," she said. "It's not
a forgotten language. Yesterday I was out riding with my children and
they were saying things in Haida. It's really nice."

Delores Churchill: The Weaver's Daughter

Even though Delores Churchill grew up the daughter of a master weaver, it wasn't until she was a forty-two-year-old bookkeeper that she first began to learn the art herself. Churchill's mother, Selina Harris Adams Peratrovich, was the teacher, a skilled woman whose traditional weavings were highly prized by collectors and cherished among the Haida people. Mrs. Peratrovich, who had learned from her mother-in-law, wove and taught until her death in 1984 at age ninety-five.

"If it wasn't for her, the art of (Haida) basketry would have died," said Churchill.

This antique Chilkat robe is part of the Alaska Museum's collection in Juneau. *(Courtesy Alaska Museum)*

Above: One of Churchill's baskets, part of the Alaska Museum's permanent collections. *(Courtesy Alaska Museum)*

Delores Churchill is a respected culture bearer who's active in teaching the skills she learned from her mother. *(Hulleah Tsinhnahjinnie)*

"No one was teaching it."

Churchill remembered entering her mother's class for her first lesson. Her mother looked up and said, "What you do here? I weave, I weave. You no look. You go home." But Churchill stayed. "She made me take my basket, undone, over and over," she said. "I didn't think I was any good." Not until several years later did Churchill find that her mother had quietly praised her abilities to other people. Still, during those first five years, Mrs. Peratrovich made Churchill burn her experimental baskets, which were not up to the master's standards, saying, "I am well-known for my baskets. If you say you learned from me, you better be good."

The legacy of Selina Peratrovich? The skills that Churchill learned from her mother, she has passed along to three daughters—Holly Churchill, April Churchill, and Evelyn Vanderhoop—now respected weavers in their own right. Meanwhile, their mother has emerged as a significant culture bearer, and people around the world have benefited from her teaching and historical research.

Today Churchill's baskets may be found in museums and private collections, and her workshops are in high demand. More than weaving alone, Churchill teaches where and how to collect the raw materials and how to properly prepare them. Honors include a Rasmuson Foundation Distinguished Artist Award, the Governor's Award for the Arts, and an Alaska State Legislative Award. In 2006, the National Endowment for the Arts named Churchill a National Heritage Fellow.

While Churchill is known as a master in Haida basketry and weaving, she also has learned techniques from master weavers in

Churchill's expertise is visible in these woven leggings. *(Courtesy Alaska Museum)*

At center, an example of traditional use of woven objects, such as a hat and cape. Left and right are close-up images of Churchill's detailed work. *(Courtesy Alaska Museum)*

other Native cultures, including how to weave the complex Chilkat robe and the rare Raven's Tail robe, part of both the Haida and Tlingit cultures. And when an ancient spruce-root hat was discovered in a glacier, the Native village of Klukwan sought Churchill's assistance to replicate the Tlingit hat that may have been five centuries old.

Cedar bark and spruce roots are commonly used materials in Churchill's art. She enjoys gathering bark and roots in the dense rain forest of Southeast, likening the forest to a cathedral. Spruce roots, properly split, dried, twisted, and woven into a basket, are best for carrying delicate foods, such as berries and clams, which might become tainted from the aromatic cedar bark. Handled correctly, stripping the bark or pulling feeder roots in the spring won't harm the tree, Churchill said.

"When we get the roots, we cover the ground back up with moss, so there's no chance of the tree being unearthed by erosion. I like to teach (students) to respect all living things . . . to be cognizant that we are the intruders," she said.

"One thing my mother always did was thank the trees, and I find myself doing it in my old age, telling the tree that I'm going to make a beautiful basket and hope it has a long life. Whenever I go out and climb the mountains now, I think of her."

Bibliography

Barker, James H. *Always Getting Ready—Upterrlainarluta: Yup'ik Eskimo Subsistence in Southwest Alaska*. Seattle: University of Washington Press, 1993.

Crowell, Aron, Gordon L. Pullar, and Amy Steffian. *Looking Both Ways: Heritage and Identity of the Alutiiq People*. Fairbanks: University of Alaska Press, 2001.

Dauenhauer, Nora Marks and Richard Dauenhauer, eds. *Haa Shuka, Our Ancestors: Tlingit Oral Narratives*. Seattle: University of Washington Press, 1987.

————. *Haa Kusteeyí, Our Culture: Tlingit Life Stories*. Seattle: University of Washington Press, 1994.

Fienup-Riordan, Ann. *Eskimo Essays: Yup'ik Lives and How We See Them*. New Brunswick, NJ: Rutgers University Press, 1990.

————. *Hunting Tradition in a Changing World: Yup'ik Lives in Alaska Today*. New Brunswick, NJ: Rutgers University Press, 2000.

Fineup-Riordan, Ann, with tranlators Alice Rearden, Marie Meade, Freda Jimmie, and Veronica Kaganak. *Yuungnaqpiallerput/The Way We Genuinely Live: Masterworks of Yup'ik Science and Survival*. Oakland, CA: Oakland Museum of California, 2007.

Fredson, John. *Haá Goodwandak: Stories Told by John Fredson to Edward Sapir*. Fairbanks: Alaska Native Language Center, 1982.

Hope III, Andrew and Thomas F. Thornton. *Will the Time Ever Come: A Tlingit Source Book*. Seattle: University of Washington Press and the Alaska Native Knowledge Network, 1993.

Kawagley, Oscar A. *A Yupiaq Worldview: A Pathway to Ecology and Spirit*. 2nd ed. Long Grove, IL: Waveland Press, 2006.

Krauss, Michael E. *In Honor of Eyak: The Art of Anna Nelson Harry*. Fairbanks: Alaska Native Language Center, 1982.

Langdon, Steve J. *The Native People of Alaska*. 4th ed. Homer, AK: Wizard Works, 2002.

Mather, Elsie. *Cauyarniuq: A Time for Drumming*. Bethel, AK: Lower Kuskokwim School District, 1985.

Meade, Marie, trans., and Ann Fienup-Riordan, ed. *The Living Tradition of Yup'ik Masks: Agayuliyararput (Our Way of Making Prayer)*. Seattle: University of Washington Press, 1996.

Mulcahy, Joanne B. and Gordon L. Pullar. *Birth and Rebirth on an Alaskan Island: The Life of an Alutiiq Healer*. Athens: University of Georgia Press, 2001.

Olson, Wallace M. *The Tlingit: An Introduction to Their Culture and History*. 3rd ed. Auke Bay, AK: Heritage Research, 1997.

Oman, Lela Kiana. *The Epic of Qayaq: The Longest Story Ever Told by My People*. Seattle: University of Washington Press, 1995.

Oozeva, Conrad, Chester Noongwook, George Noongwook, Christina Alowa, and Igor Krupnik. *Watching Ice and Weather Our Way*. Washington, DC: Arctic Studies Center, National Museum of Natural History, Smithsonian Institution, 2004.

Oswalt, Wendell H. *Bashful No Longer: An Alaskan Eskimo Ethnohistory, 1778–1988*. Norman: University of Oklahoma Press, 1990.

Pete, Shem. *Shem Pete's Alaska: The Territory of the Upper Cook Inlet Dena-ina*. Compiled and edited by James Kari. Fairbanks: Alaska Native Language Center, 1987.

Raboff, Adeline Peter. *Iñuksuk: Northern Koyukon, Gwich'in & Lower Tanana 1800-1901*. Anchorage: Alaska Native Knowledge Network, 2001.

Smith, Barbara Sweetland and Patricia J. Petrivelli. *Making it Right: Restitution for Churches Damaged and Lost During the Aleut Relocation in WWII*, Vol. 1. Anchorage: Aleutian/Pribilof Islands Association, 1993.

Swann, Brian, ed. *Voices from Four Directions: Contemporary Translations of the Native Literatures of North America*. Lincoln: University of Nebraska Press, 2004.

Wallis, Velma. *Raising Ourselves: A Gwich'in Coming of Age Story from the Yukon River*. Seattle: Epicenter Press, 2002.

———. *Bird Girl and the Man who Followed the Sun: An Athabascan Indian Legend from Alaska*. Seattle: Epicenter Press, 1996.

———. *Two Old Women: An Alaska Legend of Betrayal, Courage and Survival*. Seattle: Epicenter Press, 1993.

Web Sites

Alaskool: www.alaskool.org

Alaska Native Heritage Center: www.alaskanative.net

Alaska Native Knowledge Network: www.ankn.uaf.edu

Alaska Native Language Center, ANLC Archive: www.uaf.edu/anlc

Page locators in *italics* indicate photographs.

A

activism, 129–131

Adak, 11, 41

adaptation of Alaska Natives, 24–25, 30, 58-59, 86, 93

adze, *147*, 153, 161

Agayuliyararput (Our Way of Making Prayer) exhibit, 82–83

Agnot, Ephraim, Jr., *61*

agutak (Eskimo ice cream), 23–24

Ahmaogak, George, 98–99

Ahtna language, 17, 108

Akhiok village, *8–9*, 10-11, 55, 59, *68*, *70*

Akpik, Fanny, 91, 92

Akutan, 38, 41, 45

Alaska Eskimo Whaling Commission, 96, 102

Alaska Federation of Natives: annual convention, *2*; and cultural pride, 114–115; and politics, 31, 32; and Rural Systematic Initiative, 39; and Unanga^x (Aleut) dancers, *44*, *47*

Alaska Museum, 164–165

Alaska National Interest Lands Conservation Act (ANILCA), 33

Alaska Native Brotherhood (ANB), 31, 137

Alaska Native Claims Settlement Act (ANCSA), 31–33, 68, 78, 118

Alaska Native Heritage Festival, 49

Alaska Native Knowledge Network, 141, 168-169

Alaska Native Language Center, 37, 125, 168-169

Alaska Natives: overview, 23–25; beginnings,

25–27; contact with Europeans, 29–30, *31*; cultural revitalization, 38–39, 45, 154–155; diversity of, 7–9; homelands map, *10–11*; language affinities, 27; Native corporations, 32, 43; politics, 31–34; survival adaptations, 27–28, *28*; united but separate cultures, 34–37. *See also* specific people

Alaska Native Sisterhood, 31, 137

Alaska Indian Arts, Inc., 142

Alaska Peninsula, *11*, 12, 13, 56

Alaska Statehood Act, 31–32

alcoholism, 30

Aleutian Ballad (ship), 152

Aleutian Islands, *10*, 12, *42*

Aleuts: and diversity of Alaska Natives, 7–9; origin of term, 68. *See also* Unanga^x (Aleuts)

Alexander, Seline, *120*

Aliutor, 68

Allen, Henry, Lt., 112

Alutiiq. *See* Sugpiaq

Alutiiq Museum, 55–56, 65, 70–71

Ambler, 94

Ambrose, Hazel, *114*

Anaktuvuk Pass, *90*, 98

Anchorage Daily News, 98

Anchorage Museum, 81, 83

Angiak, Susie, *78*

Angoon, 140

angyaqs (Sugpiaq boats), 59

animal migrations, 27

Annette Island, 7, 20, 21, 149, 150, *152*

Anvik, 109, 112

Apassingok family, *84*

Aqpatat (Runner), *16*

archaeological history of

Alaskan Natives, 26–27

Arctic Slope Regional Corporation, 90

Arctic Studies Center, 59, 61–62

Arctic Village, 33, *104*, *117*

argillite carvings, 161–162

Armstrong, Karl, Jr., 67

Astrue, Father René, 78

Athabascan people: 17, 104–121. ancestral background, 109–111; birch-bark baskets, 36; cultural revitalization, 113–115; and Europeans, 111–113; fiddlers, 25, 111–112; homelands map, *10–11*, 17; linguistic groups, 105, 107, 108–109; Na-Dene ancestors, 27, 109; and subsistence, *106*, 107–108; Yukon Flats people, 116–121

Atka, 41, 45

Atu'x (Attu Island), 12, 41, 48

Ayauppiaq (Messenger Stick), *16*

B

backcountry travel, 107

baidarkas, *49*

baleen, 53, 87, *87*, 92

baleen basketry, 36, *98*

Barrow, 16, 34, 38, 90, 91, *95*, 96, 98, 100

basketry: Athabascan birch-bark baskets, 36; baleen basket, 36, *98*; Minnie Gray, *94*; spruce-root baskets, 36, 59, 68, 162; Teri Rofkar, 24; Unanga^x grass baskets, 36, 45, *50*; and Yup'ik people, *76*, 79

basket-weavers: Annie Blue, *77*; Attuan, 12, *12*; Daisy Demientieff,

109; Delores Churchill, *21*, 164–167, *165*, *167*; MaryAnn "Arnaucuaq" Sundown, *76*

beadwork, 34, 109, *120*

bearded seals, 97

bear tracks, *33*

Beaufort Sea, 89

beginnings, Alaska Natives, 25–27

Belkofski, 41

beluga whale hunting, 97

bentwood visors, 23, *42*

Bergsland, Knut, 50

Bering Sea, 14, 15, 43, 109

Bering, Vitus, (Capt.), 29

Bernhardt, Ernie, *137*

Bethel, 38, 74, 76–77, 83

bilingual education, 30

birch-bark baskets, 36, *94*

bird festival, 129

Bird Girl and the Man Who Followed the Sun (Wallis), 121

birds, importance of, 15

Birket-Smith, Kaj, 126

black shale carvings, 161–162

Blue, Annie, *77*

boarding schools, 30, 155, 160

boardwalks, *74*

bowhead whale hunting, 86, *87*, 89, 93–97, *96–97*, *98*, 100–103, *101*

Boxley, David, 153–154, 155

boyars (young boys), 101

Branch, 112

Brendible, Paul, *154*

Bristol Bay, 14, 74, 76

Broken Mammoth site, 109

Brooks Range, 89, 98, 105

Brower, Eugene, *34*

button robes, Tlingit dancers, 34

C

Calista Elders Council, 81

Camai Dance Festival, 73

Camp Pipe Spit, 94

canneries, 15, 125, 136, 152

canoes, Haida, *159*, 160, 161, *161*

Cape Espenberg, 97

Cape Krusenstern, 97

caribou, 93–94, *117*

Carlson, Barbara Švarný, 53

carving: Haida people, 20, *158*, *160*, 161–162; Nathan Jackson at work, *35*; Siberian Yup'ik carving, *85*, 86–87; Tlingit people, 19; Tsimshian people, 21, 149, 153–154, *153*, *155*; and Yup'ik people, 14, *15*, 79

Catherine II, Empress, 49

Catholic missionaries, 77, 112

Cauyarniuq (Mather), 81

cedar-bark baskets, 36

cedar carving, *153*

cedar plank housing, 139, 161

"Celebration" cultural event, *63*

celebrations. *See* potlatches

Central Yup'ik dialect, 14, 74

chadu'x (seal oil), 48

Chalkyitsik village, 30

Chandalar Valley, *39*

Charlie, Neil, 113

Chenega Bay, 56, 59

Chenega Bay Russian Orthodox Church, *58*

Chief Alexander William, *119*

Chief Charlie, 113, *119*

Chief Evan, *119*

Chief Johnson, 29

Chief Peter John, *115*

Chief Thomas, *119*

Chief William, *119*

Chignik, 59, *60*, 61

Chilkat Dancers, 142

Chilkat River, *132*, *134*

Chilkat weavings, 34, 139, *164*, 166–167, *166*, 167, *167*

chitons, gumboot, 23, 42

Christianity, 80, *80*, 162

Chugach Alaska Corporation, 56

Chugach dialect, 13

Chugach Eskimo (Sugpiaq), 13

Chukchi Sea, 89

Churchill, April, 166

Churchill, Delores, *21*, 164–167, *165*

Churchill, Holly, 166

Circle City, 117

clans: Haida people, *156*, 159; Tlingit, 134–135, 136–137, 139; and totem poles, 146; Tsimshian, 149, 152, 154

Cleveland, Grover, 7

clothing: Annie Blue, *77*; Athabascan winter clothing, *17*; Chilkat robe, 34, 139, *164*, 167; Eyak, *18*; *kuspuks*, 34, *73*; squirrel-skin parka, 62; Sugpiaq rainproof parka, *13*; Tlingit robes, *135*; wolf-fur hat, *121*; women's parkas, 28

Cold Bay, 41

Colville River, 24

commercial fishing, 43, 76, *161*, *163*

contact with Europeans, 29–30, *31*

Cook Inlet, 59, 111

Cook, Joe, *126*

copper mining, 162

Copper River, 18, 105, 111, 112, *122*

Cordova, 59, 123, 125, 127, 129

corporations, Native corporations, 32, 90

Craig, 159

Creoles, 66–67

Crowell, Aron, 59, 62

Cultural Heritage Education Institute, 113

cultural revitalization, 38–39, 45, 154–155

Cup'ik people and language, 14

D

Dall Island, 160

dancing: Camai Dance Festival, 73; "Celebration" cultural event, *63*; and cultural revitalization, 39; and diversity of Alaska Natives, 34, *36*; Iñupiat people, 98–99; Quyana Alaska celebration, *3*; Sugpiaq child, *54*; Tlingit people, *137*; Tsimshian people, *148*, 154–155, *154*; and Unanga^x (Aleut) people, *44*, *47*; Yup'ik dance masks and fans, 34, 82–83, *82*; and Yup'ik people, 14, 34, 77, 78–79

Dauenhauer, Nora and Richard, 136

Deacon, Belle, 109

Deadliest Catch (television show), 151

deer, *32*

Deg Hit'an language, 17, 108

de Laguna, Frederica, 126–127, 129, 136

Dena'ina (Tanaina) language, 17, 109

Dillingham, 15

Dirks, Moses, 50

Dirks, Moses and Larry, 23

disease. *See* epidemics

diversity of Alaska Natives, 7–9

Dixon, George, 161

dog sleds, 94

dolls, Yup'ik, *72*

drums: Iñupiat drummers, *93*; Yup'ik, *81*

Duncan, Albert, 140–141

Duncan, Pauline, 140–141

Duncan, William, 21, 149–151, 152, 154

dunlins, *127*, *129*

E

Eagle clan, Tsimshian, 155

Eagle moiety, Tlingit people, 134–135, *141*

earthquake and tsunami of 1964, 58, 65

economics and subsistence, 33–34

education: and Alaska Natives, 30, *30*; and Athabascan culture, 113–115; bilingualism and Sugpiaq people, 66; boarding schools, 30, 155, 160; Iñupiat language and culture, 91–93, 94; and Rural Systematic Initiative, 39; Tlingit language and culture, 140–141; Tuapaktusuk Culture Camp, 94; Yup'ik children, 76, 79–80

Egegik, 59

Egegik dialect, 14

Eklutna, 107

Elders: Annie Blue, *77*; and cultural revitalization, 38–39; Eyak people, 125; Haida people, 163; Iñupiat language and culture, 91–93, 103; Old Mingo cultural camp, 113–115; and preservation of heritage, 7; Sugpiaq cultural exhibit, 61–62; and Sugpiaq identity, 70–71; Tlingit people, 140; Tsimshian, 154; and Unanga^x storytelling traditions, 50–53; and Yup'ik spirit masks, 83

Elephant Point, 97

Emmonak, 78

epidemics: and contact with Europeans, 29, 136; Gwich'in people, 118; and Sugpiaq people, 64, 65

Eschscholtz Bay, 97

Eskaleuts, 27
Eskimos:and diversity of Alaska Natives, 7–9. *See also* Sugpiaq (Alutiiq)
Evanoff, Larry, 56
Evans Island, 58
Excursion Inlet, 140
The Eyak Indians of the Copper River Delta, Alaska (de Laguna and Birket-Smith), 126
Eyak Lake, *124*, 125, 127
Eyak language, 18, 125, 126, 129–130
Eyak people: 18, 122–131. Dune Lankard, 126, *128*, 129, 131; Eyak Preservation Council, 125–126; homelands map, *10–11*, *18*; Marie Smith Jones, 125, 126–127, 129–130, *130*; Na-Dene ancestors, 27; Tlingit assimilation of, 123

F

Fairbanks, 107, 119, 125
Fairbanks, Geraldine, *22*
False Pass, 41
Farciot, Charles O., 111
Far North (Iñupiat) people, 16, *16*
Fawcett, Barbara, 154
Fienup-Riordan, Ann, 81, 82–83
fish:drying herring, *22*, *78*; drying salmon, *8–9*, *114*, *116*; importance of, 15, 75
"Fishhook" village (Chalyitsik), 30
fishing: Athabascan people, *106*; Colville River, *24*; fish and game management, 33–34; fish camp, *118*; subsistence fishing, *23*, *132*, *138*; and Sugpiak people, 56–58, *56*, *57*
flooding, 78, 113
food: drying moose and

salmon, *114*; drying walrus meat, *86*; Tsimshian, 149, 153; Unanga^x foods, 48; whale meat, *87*; whale meat snack, *84*. *See also* potlatches
forced evacuation. *See* relocation
Fort Yukon, 111, 117, 121
Foster, Cecilia, 41
Four Clans longhouse, *36*, *155*
Four Clans totem, *155*
Fourth Generation Dancers, 154
four-wheelers, *91*, *107*
Frankson, Sheila, 100, 103
Friends of the Anchorage Coastal Wildlife Refuge (FAR), 53
fur parkas, *28*
Fur Rendezvous, *72*, 73
fur-sewing, 36
fur traders: Hudson's Bay Company, 111, 117–118; Russian, 12, 44–45

G

Galaktionoff, Nick, 50–51
Galena, 107
Gambell, 85, *86–87*, 96
Gambell community, 14
games, *howaq*, 55
gold, 77–78, 112
gom golth wan (thank you), 155
Goodwin, Elmer, 94
government: Athabascan tribal councils, 107; fish and game management, 33–34; tribal status and self-government, 33
Graham Island, 159, 160
grass baskets and weaving, Unanga^x , 36, 45
Grayling, 109
Gray, Minnie, *94*
Greymorning, Dr.

Stephen Neyooxet, 91–93
gumboot chitons, 23, 42
Gump, James, *81*
Gwich'in (Yukon Flats) people, 116–121, *117*, *119*, *120–121*
Gwich'in language, 17, 109

H

Haakanson, Sven, Jr., *65*, 71
Haida language, 20, 157, 159, 163
Haida people: 19–20, 156–167. carving traditions, 144; Haida Gwaii people, 159, 160; homelands map, *10–11*, *20*; leaders at Old Kasaan Potlatch, *26*; regalia, *156*; silversmithing, *37*; totem poles, *4*
Haines, 142, 144
Hän language, 17, 109
Harry, Anna Nelson, 125, 126
Hartney Bay, *127*
herring, *22*, *78*
Hewson, Wayne, 153, *153*
Holikachuk language, 17, 108
Holm, Bill, 142, 144, 153
Holy Ascension Orthodox Church, *31*, *46*
Holy Cross mission, 112
homelands map, Alaska Natives, *10–11*
Hooper Bay, 74, 75
Hooper Bay–Chevak dialect, 14
Hopson, Maligian, *97*
Hotch, Joe, *141*
houses: cedar plank housing, 139, 161; early Sugpiaq sod dwellings, 58–59; Tsimshian longhouse, 153, *155*
howaq (Sugpiaq game), 55
Howkan, 162
Huckleberry family, *38*

Hudson, Jack, 152, 153
Hudson, Ray, 50
Hudson's Bay Company, 111, 117–118
hunting: bentwood visors, 23, *42*; Iñupiat people, 89; moose hunting, *39*; seal hunting, 97; walrus hunting, 75, 86, *86*, 89, 97; whale hunting, 86, *87*, 89; Yukon Flats people, 116, *117*
Huslia, 23, 107
Hydaburg, *20*, 159, 160, 162–163

I

Ice-Age camps, 109
identity: and cultural revitalization, 38–39, 45, 154–155; Sugpiaq people, 64–71; Yup'ik people, 76
Igiugig, *112*
Ilisagvik College, 91, 92, 94
illness. *See* epidemics
Indians and diversity of Alaska Natives, 7–9
In Honor of Eyak (Krauss), 125
innovation and Alaska Natives, 24–25
Insititute of American Indian Arts, 142
Interior Alaska, 17
International Whaling Commission, 95–96
internment, Unanga^x (Aleut) people, 47
Iñupiat language, 91–94, 103
Iñupiat people: 16, 88–103. and dancing, 98–99; Eskaleut ancestors, 27; fishing, *24*; homelands map, *10–11*, *16*; Iñupiat girls, *88*; language and culture of, 91–94, 103; *Nalukataq* (blanket toss), 102–103, *102*; reindeer and caribou,

97–98, *99*; traditional homelands, 89–91, *90*; and whaling, 89, 93–97, *96–97, 98*, 100–103, *101*
Iqqaluk (Sven Haakanson, Jr.), *65*, 71
iqyax (boat), 45, 47

J

Jackson, Dorica, 147
Jackson, Mike A., 135–136
Jackson, Mona Frank, 159–160
Jackson, Nathan, *35*, 139, 140, 142–147, *143, 145, 147*
Jackson, Sheldon, 29, 97
Jackson, Stephen, 145, 147
Jacobs, Leo, 142
Jacobs, Torin Kuiggpak, 78–79
Jamachakih (Dune Lankard), 131
Jochelson, Waldemar, 50
John, Chief Peter, 115, *115*
John, Elsie, 115
John, Jerrald, *33*
John, McGarrett, *121*
Johnson O'Malley Indian Education Program, 154
Jones, Marie Smith, 125, 126–127, 129–130, *130*
Jones, William, 130
Jordan, Dick, 64
Juneau, 29, 139

K

Kaalgei (Tlingit man), *19*
Kadaagaadan (Unanga^x narrative stories), 51
Kaigani (Alsakan Haida), 19–20, 160–161
Kake, 135, 136, 159, 160
Kaktovik, 96
Kaluqaq (Iñupiat dance), 99
Kamchatka Peninsula, 68
Kamishak Bay, 59

Kanaagin, 68
Kanakanak hospital and orphanage, 15
Karluk, 59
Kasaan, 159, 162
Kasaan Bay, *162*
Kasaan Whale House, *158*
Katalla, *131*
Katmai, 65
kayaks: kayak-building class, *75*; and Sugpiaq people, *56*, 59; and Unanga^x (Aleut) people, 44, 45, 47
Kay, Sharon, *40*
KBRW radio station, 91
Kegginaqut, Kangiit-Ilu (Yup'ik Masks and the Stories They Tell) (Meade and Fienup-Riordan), 83
Kellly, Andrew, 78
kelp bulbs, *howaq* game, 55
Kenai Peninsula, 108
Ketchikan, 38, 136, 142, 144, 145, 151, 159
Kiatagmiut Eskimos, 112
Kiis Haade (separate island people), 20, 160–161
Killer Whale Clan dancing, *36*
Killer Whale hat, *141*
King Cove, 41
Kivalina, 96
Kivgiq (Messenger Feast), 16
Kivgiq festival, 98–99
Klawock, *146*, 159
Klinkwan, *20*, 140, 162
Klukwan, 132, 141
Kobuk River, 93
Kodiak, 38, 55–56, 65–66
Kodiak Island, 13, 56, 59, *62. See also* Sugpiaq (Alutiiq) people
Koiandlas, 162
Koniag dialect, 13
Koniag Eskimo (Sugpiaq), 13
"Koniag shareholders," 68

Kotzebue, 16, 38, 90, 97
Kotzebue Elders, 94
Kotzebue Sound, 89
Koyukon language, 17, 23, 109
Koyukuk River, 105, 112
Krauss, Dr. Michael, 125, 126, 130
Kupreanoff Point, 59
Kupreanof Island, 136
Kuskokwim River, 73, 74, 77, 78, 105, 111
kuspuks, 34, *73*
Kvichak River, *112*
Kwigilingok, *74*

L

lakes region, Southwestern Alaska, 113
land claims lawsuit, 137
land use, 29
language: Alaska Native Language Center, 37; Athabascan, 108–109, 114; as cultural distinction, 37; and cultural identity, 64–71; and cultural revitalization, 38–39; Iñupiat people, 91–94; language affinities, 27; Sugpiaq naming practices, 70; Yup'ik people, 74, 79–80. *See also* specific languages
Lankard, Dune, 126, *128*, 129, 131
Laroyen family, *17*
Larsen Bay, 59
Laurence, Ted, 142
Leask, Chris, *148*
Leask, Melody, *148*, 154
Lekanof, Agnes and Anna, *29*
Lekanoff-Gregory, Patricia, 42, *42*, 47
Lethin, David, 151–152
Little Diomede, 96
longhouse, Tsimshian, 153, *155*
Long Island, 160
Looking Both Ways (Pullar, Crowell, and Steffian, eds.), 71

Lower Cook Inlet, 13
Lower Kalskag, *80*
lustu'x (pickled sea lion flipper), 48

M

maktak (whale blubber), 100
Malutin, Susan, 62
Marks, Horace, 142
masks: Sugpiaq masks, *13*, 65, 71, *71*; and Yup'ik people, 14; Yup'ik spirit masks, 77, 82–83, *82*
Masset, 159
Matanuska River Valley, 111
Matanuska-Susitna Valley, 94
Matfay, Elder Larry, 55
Mather, Casper, *21*
Mather, Elsie, 81
Mayo, Alfred, 111
Mayo, Will, 32–33, 113–115
McIntyre, Marcella, 155
McIntyre, Theo, 149, 154, 155
Meade, Marie, 83
Melodevoff, Tim D., Jr., 67
Merculieff, Larry, *43*
Messenger Feast, *16*
Metlakatla Choral Society, *151*
Metlakatla community, 20, 21, 149–155, *150*
Minto Flats, 113
missionaries, 29–30, *31*, 76–77, 80, 149–151, 152, 154
Molly Hootch Act, 30
moose, *39, 114*
moosehide regalia, 34
Moravian missionaries, 76
More Than Words (film), 130
Mountain Village, 83
Mount Novarupta, 65
Mumtrekhlogamiut (Bethel), 76–77
music, Athabascan fiddlers, *25*, 112

N

Nacktan, Lena, 125
Na-Dene Indians, 27, 109, 140
Nalukataq (blanket toss), 102–103, *102*
National Science Foundation, 39
Natkong, Clara, 163
Naumoff, Alfred, 56
Nayamin, Natalia, *72*, 73
Nayamin, Rebecca, *72*, 73
Nelson Lagoon, 41
New Kasaan, 162
"New Metlakatla," 149, *151*
Nikolski, 41
1964 earthquake and tsunami, 58, 65
Ninilchik, *108*
Nome, 16
Nondalton, *113*
nondiscrimination act, 30
non-Natives and Native corporations, 32
North Alaskan Iñupiat dialect, 16
North Slope, 32, 78, 89, 97
North Slope Borough, 90
North Slope Borough School District, 91–93
Norton Sound dialect, 14
nose labret, *131*
Nuchalawoya site, 111
Nuchek Island, 56
Nuiqsut, 24, 96
Nulato mission, 112
Nunapitchuk, 83
Nuniaqmiut (people of Old Harbor), 70
Nunivak dialect, 14
Nushagak community, 15
Nushagak men, *14*
Nuuciq Spirit Camp, 56
Nuyaagiq (Dr. Stephen Neyooxet Grey-morning), 91–93

O

oil, 32, 78, 97
Oktollik, Calvin and Irma, 100
Old Harbor, 59, 65, 70

Old Kasaan Potlatch, *26*
Old Minto, 113
Old-Time Fiddling Festivals, *25*, 112
Old Togiak, 77
Old Town, 125
Olson, Nina, 71
Olson, Wallace M., 136
Onion Portage, 93
oral history and tradition: and cultural revitalization, 38–39; and Unanga^x people, 51–53; Yup'ik people, 76
Orion's Belt, 53
Ouzinkie, 59

P

Pacific Eskimo (Sugpiaq), 13
pack ice, *92*, *95*, 100, 102
Paddy, Albert, *132*
Pahl, Faye, *125*
Paktotak, Elise, 98
Paleoindians, 27
Patkotak, James, 91
Patkotak, Simeon, Sr., *98*
Paukan, Andy, 83
Pauloff Harbor, 41
Paul, William, 137
Peratrovich, Selina Harris Adams, 164–165, 167
Perez, Juan, 161
Peterson, Phyllis, *66*
petroglyphs, *62*
Pinart, Alphonse, 71
plank housing, 139
Point Barrow, *92*
Point Hope, 16, *91*, 93, 96, 100, 103
politics, 31–34
Port Heiden, 59
Port Lions, 59
Port Moller, 59
potlatches: and cultural revitalization, 37, 130–131; Eyak people, 130–131; Old Kasaan Potlatch, *26*; Tlingit people, 19; Tsimshian people, 21; Yup'ik people, 73, 77, 78, 79

Pribilof Islands, 12, 41, *42*
Prince of Wales Island, 140, *146*, 159, 160, 161, *162*
Prince William Sound, 13, 18, 59, 65
Project Jukebox, 76
Prospect Creek, 111
Protection of the Theotokos Chapel, 68
Prudhoe Bay oil field, 32
Pullar, Gordon, 59, 64, *64*, 71
Pullar, Gordon, Jr. "Gordy," 65–66
pumyaa (encore), 79

Q

qasgiq (men's house), 83
Qawalangin Tribe of Unalaska, 48
Qik'rtarmuit (people of the island), 70
Qong qons (Great Month), 161
Queen Charlotte Islands, 20, 160
Quinhagek, 78
qungaayu'x (humpback salmon hump), 48
Quyana Alaska celebration, *3*, *51–52*

R

Raising Ourselves (Wallis), 121
Rampart, 111
the Raven character, 37
Raven moiety, Tlingit people, 134–135
Raven's Tail robe, 139, 167
red cedar, *32*
Red Dog Mine, 97
reindeer herding, 97–98, *99*
religion: Holy Ascension Orthodox Church, *31*; and Yup'ik people, 78. *See also* Christianity; Russian Orthodox Church
relocation: Haida people,

20; Sugpiaq people, 65; Tsimshian people, 7
reparation, 28, 38, 47
Richards, Lucy, 92
ringed seals, 97
"Ring of Fire," 41
robes, 36
Rofkar, Teri, 24
Rose Urban Rural Exchange, 94
Rossing, Anton, 67
Rossing, Olga Vasilie, 67
Rossing, Vasili Shmakov, 67
Rural Systematic Initiative, 39
Russian fur traders, 12, 44–45, 123
Russian Orthodox Church: cemetery and chapel, *49*; at Chenega Bay, *58*; Holy Ascension Orthodox Church, *31*, *46*, 47; Protection of the Theotokos Chapel, 68; and Sugpiaq people, 66; and Yup'ik people, 76, *80*
Russian Orthodox Mission, 15
Russian settlers: on Kodiak Island, 65, 66–68; and Tlingit people, 136; and Yup'ik people, 76
rye grass basketry, *12*

S

salmon: Athabascan people, *106*; carving, *153*; Copper River, *122*, 123–124; drying moose and salmon, *114*, *116*. *See also* fishing
Sand Point, 41
San gias (Killer Whale Month), 161
Sarychev, Gavriil Andreevich, 49
Savoonga, 14, 85, 96
Savoonga man and children, *15*

Saxman, 147

Saxman Totem Park, 142

Scandinavians, *66*, 97–98

Schieffelin brothers prospecting trip, 111

Schleusner, Carla, *148*

scrimshaw, 36

sea eggs (sea urchins), 42, 69

Sealaska Heritage Insititute, 140, 151

seal intestines, rainproof parka, *13*

seals on St. Paul Island, *43*

sea mammals: importance of, 15; and Iñupiat people, 93; and *Nalukataq* (blanket toss), *102*, 103; reliance of Yup'ik people on, 75

sea otters, 44–45, 55

sea urchins, 42, *69*

self-identity and self-esteem, 30, 39, 49

Seward Peninsula, 89, 91, 97–98

Seward Peninsula Iñupiat dialect, 16

sewing, 36, 62, *77*, 89

Shangukeidi brothers, *19*

"shareholders" and Native corporations, 68

Sheldon Jackson College, 103

Sheldon Jackson Museum, 83

Shelikhov, Gregorii, 65

shkeek (Eagle), 155

Shmakov, Ivan, 67

Shmakov, Vasili, 67

Siberian Yup'ik language, 15

Siberian Yupik people, 13, 15, 84–87, *84–87*

silversmithing, *37, 140*

Sinate, Fort Yukon Indian Chief, *111*

Sitka, 83, 140, 142, 160

Sitka black-tailed fawn, *32*

skin-sewing, 36, 62, 77, 79

smallpox epidemics, 64, 65

Smith, Pam, 126

Smithsonian Institution, 59, 61–62

sobriety, 30, 119, 129

sod houses, Sugpiaq, 58–59

Soonagrook, William, Jr., *85*

Southcentral Alaska, 17

spruce-root baskets, 36, 59, 68, 162

spruce-root hat, 167

SS Delarof (ship), 27

Stevens, Scar and Minnie, 127

Stevens, Sophie, 127, 129

Stevens Village, 107

St. George, *29*, 41

St. Lawrence Island, 14, 85, *87*

St. Mary's Mission, 77, 78

stone tools, 26

Stories Out of Slumber (Hudson), 50

storytelling: and Alaskan Natives, 28; and cultural distinction, 37; Haida people, 163; and totem poles, 146; and the Unanga'x people, 48–53

St. Paul, 41, *43*

subsistence lifestyle: and Alaskan Natives, *23*, 24–25; Athabascan people, 17, *106*, 107–108, 119, 121; Eyak people, 18; Iñupiat people, *90*, 93–97, *96–97*; and politics, 33–34, *34*; Tlingit people, *132, 138*; and Yup'ik dolls, *72*, 73; Yup'ik people, 14, 74–76

Sugpiaq (Alutiiq) people: 13, 54–71. cultural artifacts exhibition, 59, 61–62; cultural identity essay, 63–71; Eskaleut ancestors, 27; fishing and seafaring

heritage, 56–58, *56, 57*; homelands map, *10–11*; Igiugig, *112*; Sugpiaq child, *59*; territory and communities of, 59

Sugt'stun language, 13, 59, 71

suicide, 30

Sukkwan Island, 160, 162

Sun'aqmiut (people of Kodiak), 70

Sundown, MaryAnn "Arnaucuaq," *76*

survival adaptations, 27–28, *28*

Susitna River, 105

Švarný, Gertrude Hope, 48, 53

Švarný, Samuel, 48

Swaatk'i (Tlingit man), *19*

Sweeden, Agnes, *72*, 73

Sx'anduoo (Tlingit man), *19*

T

Taku tribe, 29

Tanacross, 113

Tanacross language, 17, 109

Tanana, 111, 115

Tanana Chiefs Conference, 32, 113, *119*

Tanana language, 17, 109

Tanana River, 105, 109, 111, 112

Tangirnaq (Woody Island), *64*, 67

Tan'icak (Gordon Pullar), 59, 64, *64*, 71

Tatitlek, 59, 62

Taya'ut, 68

temperature extremes, 111

"Three Large Men Looking Down" (Orion's Belt), 53

tidepools, *67*

Tikigaq High School, 103

Tlingit–Haida Central Council, 29, 31, 157

Tlingit language, 19

Tlingit people, 19, 132–147; attempts to regain land, 29; and carving tradition, *35, 136*, 139–140, *139, 140*, 142–147, *143, 146*; and cultural pride, 137–139, 141; homelands map, *10–11, 19*; Na-Dene ancestors, 27; social organization of, 134–136; Tlingit dancers, 34. *See also* Haida people

Togiagamute, 77

Togiak, 78

Toksook Bay, 82–83

Tolovana River, 113

Tongass National Forest, 29, 31

tools: adze, *147*, 153; stone tools, 26

totem poles: Haida people, *4*, 20, *158, 160*; Nathan Jackson at work, *35*; Tlingit carving tradition, *35, 136*, 139–140, *139, 140*, 142–147, *143, 146*

trade networks, 27

trans-Alaska pipeline, 27

tribal claims and sovereignty, 32–33

tribal councils, Athabascan, 107

Tsimshian language, 21

Tsimshian people: 20–21, 148–155. carving traditions, 144, 152, *153, 155*; clans of, 149, 152; dancing, *148*, 154–155, *154*; homelands map, *10–11, 21*; Huckleberry family, *38*; Metlakatla community, 20, 21, 149–155, *150*; relocation of, 7; Tsimshian woman wearing traditional regalia, *6*

Tuapaktusuk Culture Camp, 94

tuberculosis, 27

tundra boardwalks, *74*

Tununak, *22*

Tunusan (Unanga^x life accounts), 51

Tutada (to listen), 53

Twin Hills village, 78, *79*

Two Old Women (Wallis), 121

U

uda'x (dry fish), 48

Ukpeagvik (Barrow), 90

umiaks (Iñupiat boat), 90, 100

Unalakleet River, 74, 91

Unalaska, 38, 41, *46*, 48

Unangam Tunuu language, 12, 45, 50

Unangam Ungiikangin kayux Tunusangin (Aleut Tales and Narratives) (Jochelson), 50

Unanga^x (Aleut) people: 12, 40–53. boatmaking skills, 45, 47, *49*; and dancing, *44*, *47*, *51–52*; Eskaleut ancestors, 27; evacuation of villages during World War II, *29*; homelands map, *10-11*, *12* ; influence on non-Natives on, *48*; profile of, 48–53; and Russian fur traders, 44–45; and Russian Orthodox Church, *46*, 47, *49*; and subsistence, 41–43, *43*; and Sugpiaq people, 68

Unga, 41

Unga Island, *40*, 41

Ungiikan (Unanga^x stories), 48, 49–50, 51–53

united but separate cultures, 34–37

University of Alaska:Oral History Program, 76; and

Rural Systematic Initiative, 39

University of Alaska Fairbanks, 71

University of Alaska Press, 61

Upper Kuskokwim language, 17, 109

Upper Tanana language, 17, 109

V

Vanderhoop, Evelyn, 166

Van Hatten, Amy, 107–108

Veniaminov, Ivan, 45

villages and Athabascan culture, 108–109

W

Wainwright, 93, 96

Wales, 96

Wallace, John, 140

Wallis, Velma, 116, 121

walrus: hunting, 75, 86, *86*, 89, 97; Siberian Yup'ik carving, *15*, *85*, 86

waterborne travel and commerce, 43–44

weather patterns, 27

weaving: Chilkat weavings, 34, 139, *164*, 166–167, *166*, *167*; Haida people, 20; leggings, *166*; Teri Rofkar, 24; Tlingit people, 19, 139–140

western sandpipers, *127*, *129*

whalebone and walrus ivory figure, *15*

whale hunting, *34*, 37; and Iñupiat people, 89, 93–97, *96–97*, *98*, 100–103, *101*

whale meat snack, *84*

Whywah (Let's go!), 154

Williams, Paul, *119*

woodworking, 36

Woody Island, *64*, 67

"Word of the Day", KBRW radio station, 91

World War II, 27, *29*, 30, 47

X

'xani'gilix (sun's afterglow), 53

Y

Yindayaank' (Tlingit man), *19*

Yukon Delta National Wildlife Refuge, 75

Yukon Flats people, 116–121, *117*, *119*, *120–121*

Yukon–Kuskokwim Delta, 14

Yukon River, 74, 77, 78, 105, 111, 112, 117

Yup'ik people: 14–15, *14–15*, 72–83. contact with Westerners, 76–77, 80; cosmology and worldview, 26, 80–81; cultural identity, 73–76, 78–79; Eskaleut ancestors, 27; homelands map, *10–11*, *14*; waterways and boat travel, 75–76, *75*; Yup'ik dance masks, 82–83, *82*; Yup'ik dolls, *72*

Yuungnaqpiallerput (Yup'ik museum exhibition), 81

Z

Zeeder, Elder S., Sr., *8–9*

Zeeder, Stella, *69*

zinc mining, 97